LIVING
FOR ULTIMATE IMPACT

Gil Hodges

LIVING

FOR ULTIMATE IMPACT

Living from Heaven,
So You Can Bring Heaven to Earth

Gil Hodges

Kingdom Equipping Center
7191 Grashio Dr.
Colorado Springs, CO 80920

KingdomTalksMedia.com
(719) 464-4873

ACKNOWLEDGMENTS

To all those who made this possible:

My beautiful Wife – Adena Hodges, who did the majority of the editing
Lilly Weaks – First-stage Editor
J.P. Brooks – Final Editor, who pulled it all together

My Team at Kingdom Equipping Center, for their input:

Karen Britt – Cover Design
Mindy Upton – Executive Assistant
Eric Upton – Technical Director
Muriel Weidemann – Show Assistant, who wrote the bio
Lisa Perez Benitez – Content Writer, who wrote the summary
Michael Tulk – Master of Show Notes

All of you had valuable input. Thank you!

Contents

Preface

I share this book with you because as I made the shift described within these pages, it changed my life for good, forever. It can change your life, too.

These pages contain no secrets, but rather mysteries: mysteries hidden from us only because we didn't know where to search. This book is a path to those mysteries. I hope they lead you to freedom, as they did me.

I'd like to acknowledge my wonderful wife, Adena Hodges, and my children who lived with me through many tough years spiritually, mentally, emotionally, and financially. If only I had known earlier what I know now.

Forward

There are many wonderful, overarching themes to discover in the Scriptures. One, of course, is the central theme of redemption through the Messiah, Jesus Christ. That topic is prophesied from the first book, Genesis, then fulfilled in the gospels, and finally experienced in the rest of the canon of Scripture. And as an offshoot of the redeeming work of Jesus, we get another crucial theme. This one is exposed only after Jesus fulfills His earthly ministry and fills the believers with power. The secondary central theme is this:

You, too, can do all the amazing things you've read about in the Bible!

I imagine that people living in Old Testament times looked on with awe and appreciation at those special, individually called people who were carrying out God's mighty works. I can imagine the man on the street in Israel being extremely thankful that a judge, prophet, or king was around to carry out those great exploits. Sure, Moses could part the Red Sea, Samson could defeat the Philistines, and Elijah could call down fire from heaven, but that's only the business of those who are specially called and anointed for that purpose, right? No. It's not that God wasn't *offering* a more inclusive relationship with His otherworldly power, it's just that humanity often wasn't ready to receive it. (See the Israelites' decisions while wandering in the desert.)

But everything changed the minute Jesus ascended into the heavens and released the Holy Spirit to the earth. From that moment on, every single person who has received the Spirit became just like those heroes of the faith. Supernatural power is now available to all of us. Healings, miracles, and even ascensions to heaven have now become standard operating procedure for everyone who calls on the name of the Lord.

And that's why the book you are holding right now is so important.

Gil wrote this book so that you don't count yourself out; so you don't assume that the greatness of God's kingdom is to be experienced only by someone else. This book pushes you to take hold of this amazing truth without waiting until you feel that you're up to the task.

It was written just for you. Right now. Just as you are. Think of it as a giant permission slip to pursue all that God has for you!

— Christopher Paul Carter
www.discoveringtheheavens.org
Author of *Cosmic Shift* and
In the Palaces of Heaven

Introduction

*"Stand fast, therefore, in the
liberty by which Christ has made us
free, and do not be entangled again
with a yoke of bondage."*
Galatians 5:1

We all have a story. I won't share all the shameful and ugly details of my life—just enough so you get the idea. As so many people do, I used my story to gain sympathy and attention. My past had become my identity. My sad story was who I thought I was. If I needed attention, I would subconsciously find a reason to share my story so I could get that attention.

But now I see my story as the building blocks of character that have made me who I am today. I have no desire to get attention for what I now look back on as simply the challenging times that made me strong. I also have no desire to dishonor anyone, especially my parents, whom I consider the true heroes of my life.

I was in my fifties when I finally found freedom from a lifelong battle with depression, negative thoughts, and a deeply toxic religious way of thinking that crippled my ability to see who I really was and my purpose in this world. For decades I had gone to counselors and inner healing ministries such as Elijah House, Sozo, Theophostics, and psychiatrists, all in an effort to get some level of relief from my pain. They did help to some degree, but they never gave me the full freedom I desired. I repeatedly told my wife, Adena, not merely that I hated myself (the self I thought I was, that is), but that I *loathed* my life.

> ***I was in my fifties when***
> ***I finally found freedom***
> ***from a lifelong battle***
> ***with depression.***

Several counselors told me that I had some of the worst life scenarios they had ever heard. As a result, I didn't value myself—to put it mildly. I suffered through so many life situations that caused me to believe I was a worthless piece of trash. I was told over and over again, "I wish you had never been born!" At a young age I came to believe that my life was meaningless and I was only in everyone's way. So when I was a teenager, I attempted suicide. I put a loaded revolver to my head and pulled the trigger. Thankfully, when I had cocked the revolver, the lone bullet rotated out of firing position, so it didn't fire when I pulled the trigger. I then lost my nerve.

Set Free for Ultimate Impact

It wasn't until years later, when I began to sit and listen (meditate on) and allow Father to speak to me, that my healing journey truly began. And I had to *choose* to take these actions. I had to choose not only to listen to what Father was saying to me and about me, but I had to really struggle and fight to *receive* it—to actually believe it and let it begin to redefine who I thought I was and to truly change me. This was the beginning of my breakthrough.

> ### *I had to choose not only to listen to what Father was saying to me and about me, but I had to actually believe it!*

Then, as I grew in my understanding of what the phrase "seated with Christ in Heavenly places"[1] truly means and all the implications of it, this truth began to change my life. Also that we are told to "come boldly to the throne of grace."[2]

As I began to believe in who the Bible and Father told me I was, Father began to open up to me new revelation regarding these verses, and all of Scripture. The Bible came alive with new truth and a new depth of understanding that began to set me free even further. He'll do the same for you, too, as you persevere to accept the truth and truly believe it.

As Adena and I began to share these insights at the church we were pastoring at the time, we saw the power and impact these truths had on the lives of others. People began coming to us and asking us so many questions, we realized that we needed to put these teachings and revelations into a discipleship course that was accessible to everyone. So we eventually did; it's called "Ultimate Impact." Once you are set free by these teachings and revelations, you will be ready to have your ultimate impact on the earth! You can find this course on our website at:
www.kingdomtalksmedia.com.

I can tell you from personal experience, it doesn't matter how deep your pain or how traumatic your life has been—you can and will be set free! The deed is done! Jesus came to set you free, and He succeeded! One of my favorite verses now is Galatians 5:1:

It is for freedom that Christ has set us free.

And you do have the freedom to choose what you believe. Each and every one of us, in fact, *have* to choose what we will believe. You can choose to believe what the world has told you about yourself, OR you can begin the awesome adventure and journey of truth and discover who you really are! You get to step into what Jesus has already done for you, and this book will show you the way.

In these pages, you will find the truths that have set me free. My heart's desire for you is that you will experience freedom in ways you never have before, and that this will be the beginning of walking out an entirely new life: a life full of the love, joy, and peace that Father intends for you to have.

* * * * *

(NOTE: Throughout this book I will use the term *mature sons* or *maturing sons*. This is not a gender-exclusive term. It refers to all the children of God growing up to be like Jesus. And as others have said, if we men have to relate to being part of the bride of Christ, then it should be okay for women to relate to being a son.)

Chapter One

The Two Trees

Which tree are you living from?

The greatest expression of God's love to us is His gift of free will. True love cannot manifest without a free choice, and God did not want robots, but people made in His image, to rule and reign with Him.

To give Adam and Eve this freedom to choose, God placed two trees in the garden—the Tree of Life and the Tree of the Knowledge of Good and Evil. In Scripture, we only get the "Cliff notes" version: the basic facts. For example, we don't know how long it was before Adam and Eve sinned, but it could easily have been years, decades, or even centuries.

Like most people, I used to look at the story of the two trees as a simple story of disobedience. But what did those trees really represent? When we dig a little deeper, the story takes on a whole new meaning. It turns out that it's not simply about a choice made by our first parents some 6,000 years ago—in one way or another, you and I are making that very same choice, every day of our lives.

The fact is, even to this day, we *all* live out our lives under the influence of those two trees. And we all get to choose which tree we want to live out of.

> **We all live out our lives under the influence of those two trees.**

Our entire world, especially the Western mindset, is deeply steeped in the fruit of the Tree of Knowledge. We see this clearly when even committed Christians choose to value knowledge and being right so highly, that they blithely ignore Jesus's command to love and treat the other person as they themselves would want to be treated. Instead, they insistently drive home their point in order to prove that *they* are right and the other person is wrong; to prove that they are *superior* to the other person in knowledge, discernment, wisdom, and doctrine. But this is nothing more nor less than sinful pride. Some even go so far as to ostracize anyone who doesn't agree with them perfectly, even in minor details. This is why there are so many denominations in our Western "Christianized" world.

This is the fruit of the Tree of Knowledge - pride, putting others down in order to build ourselves up, broken relationships, and more.

So as you can see, the two trees stood for much more than a simple choice of obedience versus disobedience.

The Tree of Life represented a relationship with Father. And our loving Father would not have withheld anything good from Adam and Eve, nor all of mankind. I believe that they, and we, would have learned all that we wanted to learn, in time, and in relationship with Him. After all, Heaven is all about relationship, and He is a loving Father.

The Tree of Knowledge was not merely about being disobedient: it represented the selfish and prideful choice to skip the relationship process and simply grab what I want and grab it now.

Satan deceived Adam and Eve into thinking that they could instantly get all the knowledge they wanted and become like God! The saddest part to me is that they chose to forego a loving, intimate relationship with their Father in order to have mere knowledge: knowledge that they thought would make them like Him. The reality was that they were *already* like God, made in His image. They were deceived into reaching for something that they already had. How often do we do the same thing?

God is love, and "whoever does not love does not know God, because God is love."3 Jesus was quite clear what the greatest commandments are: "'Love the Lord your God with all your heart and with all your soul and with all your mind.' This is the first and greatest commandment. And the second is like it: 'Love your neighbor as yourself'."[4] And Jesus's new commandment, "Love one another. As I have loved you, so you must love one another. By this everyone will know that you are my disciples, if you love one another."[5]

It's amazing, but I don't see knowledge *anywhere* in the Top Ten of God's laws. Yet tragically, most Christians obviously value knowledge and being right far above learning how to love one another. Why is this?

> **Most Christians obviously value knowledge and being right far above learning how to love one another.**

The simple answer? Pride. Pride is one of the most sinister and subtle of evils. It teaches us how to package our self-centered desires in beautiful language and reasoning so we can justify doing what we want…rather than doing what is good and right according to the laws of Heaven (i.e., rather than truly loving other people, and treating them as we want to be treated).

The bottom line to me on this issue is that the Tree of Life represents **living from love in**

relationship. It is living to the max by giv
max. If we all did this, there would be ı
anything for anyone. Jesus gave His max on tne
Cross. He gave His life. And He asks no less from
us. He says, "Whoever wants to be my disciple
must deny themselves and take up their cross
daily and follow me."[6] Wow! What a contrast from
our world, which teaches us that knowledge is
power and that it's perfectly acceptable to alienate,
demean, and dominate our fellow human beings in
order to gain that power.

Learning to love means giving others the
freedom to choose, just as God gives it to us. Most
people, however, want to control and manipulate
others into their point of view or under their
dominion. This is never God's way. He lovingly
gives us choices, and He asks each of us to
lovingly extend that same right to others. This is so
counter-intuitive to our way human way of thinking
and acting. This is why the Father said, "My
thoughts are not your thoughts, nor are your ways
My ways. For as the heavens are higher than the
earth, so are My ways higher than your ways, and
My thoughts than your thoughts."[7]

It can be easy for us to read these verses from
a Tree of Knowledge perspective, as if God is
simply gloating about His moral and intellectual
superiority as we humans so often do. He's not.
He's inviting us to shift our mindset from a right vs.

wrong, prideful, "I'm smarter and better than you so I get to control you" attitude to a loving relationship with our Father, where we humbly acknowledge that we are *not* all-knowing or all-righteous, and we instead learn from him how to think and judge and treat others.

Now ask yourself this:

Are you living from the Tree of Life, or from the Tree of Knowledge? Do you live to give and love? Is this your primary mode of operation? Are you all about developing close relationships and learning to love better in those relationships? Do you press through in difficult relational challenges? Or do you bail out and find a reason to move on without learning the lesson? Do you find yourself more often than not fighting to be right? Wanting to know more than others so you can keep the upper hand on those around you? Do you humbly and lovingly lift others up? Or do seek knowledge for the purpose of feeding an inner desire for acclaim and superiority over others, whether out of pride or fear?

If you are seeking knowledge over relationship, my friend, then you've made the same choice that Adam and Eve did.

And I'll be open with you. If I don't constantly keep my eyes on Jesus and on seeking an intimate relationship with Him, I easily slide right back into my place of pride and wanting to be

> ***If you are seeking knowledge over relationship, my friend, then you've made the same choice that Adam and Eve did.***

right. I want to be lifted up as the one to follow. I want all the right answers, so I can be smarter and looked up to.

So, speaking for myself, by God's grace I will live to lift up Jesus—instead of myself and my self-righteousness. I will learn to love others as He does—from a heart of true humility and selfless love, sacrificing my right to be right, to be in charge, to be acclaimed as superior.

Chapter Two

The Enemy Within

Pride will keep you from being who you are called to be.

Do you want to make an impact in the world? I believe that in our innermost being we all want to do good, to see a change for the better. If we could, we would live our lives in such a way as to have our ultimate impact. We would all make the greatest and best difference we possibly could. This is in the heart of every person, though it's buried deeply in some. Do you know why everyone wants this? Because God created that desire in us, in the very fiber of our being. We were all meant to be world-changers!

In 2014, God put a message in my heart. I was driving home from a meeting and I felt His presence fill my car. He began downloading into my spirit this message. I felt like He said:

"Gil, in order for Me to have My ultimate impact in a church, a city, a region, and the world, there need to be apostles, prophets, teachers, pastors, and evangelists who come together and create training and equipping centers which will

help My people understand who they really are and how to mature into sons who look like Jesus! They need to know their destinies, their scrolls, because I've already written their destinies out for them![8]

"When My people are willing and able to humbly take up their destiny and position, and serve Me and their brothers and sisters with whom I've placed them, they will be more fulfilled than if they were to get all the things the world offers them and tells them will bring them happiness. Those things will not bring them happiness, but the fulfillment of their destiny will!

"Once my people come together in humility and love for one another and operate as one body, then I will have My ultimate impact in a church, a city, a region, and the world."

Why haven't we been able to have the ultimate impact that God intended? What is holding us back? Many people look at external issues, but it really begins within us. Often our

Why haven't we been able to have the ultimate impact that God intended?

biggest hindrance is a blind spot we can't see in ourselves, although we might see it in others.

The greatest hindrance that the body of Christ faces is the same as it's always been. It's the first item on God's list of seven things that He hates more than anything else. What is it? Pride! Pride leads to arrogance, which leads to lording it over others, which steals their freedom. But Jesus gave His *life* for everyone's freedom![9]

Because pride is such a powerful evil and has such terrible consequences, the enemy does what he does whenever there is any move of God—he uses pride to cause some of us to start trying to hold on to what God gave them, as if it were only for them. Their focus shifts from feeding and giving to the body of Christ what it needs for the next season, to "How do I take care of myself?" And in some cases, it becomes simply about money, power, or control. (To be clear, money itself is not the enemy. Money is not evil and is fine to have, but the *love* of money can, and has, caused many to veer off the narrow path.[10])

How sad that we, the children of God, haven't matured to the point where we can get past our pride and insecurities and carry out the will of our Father! So let's keep an open heart and open mind as we move forward.

As I write this book, one of my greatest desires is to see the mission of the Ephesians 4 fivefold ministry completed.

> And He gave the apostles, the prophets, the evangelists, the shepherds, and teachers, to equip the saints for the work of ministry, for building up the body of Christ, until we all attain to the unity of the faith and of the knowledge of the Son of God, to mature manhood, to the measure of the stature of the fullness of Christ, so that we may no longer be children, tossed to and fro by the waves and carried about by every wind of doctrine, by human cunning, by craftiness in deceitful schemes. Rather, speaking the truth in love, we are to grow up in every way into him who is the head, into Christ, from whom the whole body, joined and held together by every joint with which it is

> equipped, when each part is working
> properly, makes the body grow so that
> it builds itself up in love.[11]

I dare say that the Church has not come anywhere near full unity, nor are we walking in the full power and authority of Jesus! So we clearly still need the ministry of these five different types of ministers.

But many of us have been wounded by twisted understandings of leadership, where it is all about a ministry or person lording it over everyone else. However, the true form of leadership that Jesus exemplified is based on love, freedom, and lifting others up.

Some will say that we *are* complete in Christ: that our fullness was fully accomplished in Him. And I say, yes indeed! But we are still working out the transformation of our minds so that we can walk it out in the earth realm. If our completeness was already accomplished by Jesus, then why did Paul write about the 5-fold ministry thirty years after Jesus's death? Jesus *did* accomplish everything in Himself. But we have to take hold of it. We *are* free! We *are* delivered! We *are* fully empowered! But we haven't fully believed it yet or known how to walk it out.

So let's take a look at what each of us can do to help pull the body of Christ together, rather than participate in the enemy's scheme to rip us apart.

* * * * *

Truly we are living in a powerful, exciting, and intriguing time: the time after the resurrection. Why is our era so amazing? Because Scripture says that Jesus was the first fruit of those who would follow Him. **This means that God wants you to be like Jesus!** We are all supposed to "be Jesus" to everyone we meet!

Now it took God in the flesh, Jesus, to show us how this is done. And He did it in human form, with no advantage over us—except that He knew it was attainable. The power and authority that Jesus displayed? He said that we would have the same—but even greater![12]

When we are in right alignment with Father's will, seeking His Kingdom first, seeking Him first, and loving Him "with all your heart and with all your soul and with all your mind,"[13] **then** "these signs will accompany those who believe: In my name they will drive out demons; they will speak in new tongues; they will pick up snakes with their hands; and when they drink deadly poison, it will not hurt them at all; they will place their hands on sick people, and they will get well."[14]

How do we attain this?

Jesus made it plain. Seek first His kingdom and His righteousness - His way of acting and living - and all these other things will be given to us.15 But the only way to experience His kingdom and His righteousness is through a living, active relationship with Him. The deeper the relationship, the more of His Kingdom power He'll entrust us with.

The Father is *all* about relationship. This is why it's **love** that conquers all. Jesus was clear: "By this everyone will know that you are my disciples, **if you love one another.**"16

The Father **is** love, so love is priority number one to Him!

Here's a great passage to meditate on. Ask the Father to cause these truths to soak into every fiber of your being.

> "God is love. Whoever lives in love lives in God, and God in them. This is how love is made complete among us, so that we will have confidence on the day of judgment: In this world we are like Jesus. There is no fear in love. But perfect love drives out fear, because fear has to do with punishment. The one who fears is not made perfect in love. We love because He first loved us. Whoever claims to love God yet hates a brother or sister is a liar. For whoever does not love their brother and sister,

> whom they have seen, cannot love God,
> whom they have not seen."[17]

This is Kingdom! Love permeates all of Heaven and all of the Kingdom, and it supersedes everything else including what we think we know about scripture and God (i.e. Tree of Knowledge)

> ***Love supersedes everything else including what we think we know about scripture and God (i.e. Tree of Knowledge)***

But our pride and arrogance of being "right" has caused so much division, that Christians are far too often merely *preaching* love, but actually living out the opposite. Our interpretation of Scripture (and in some cases, our spiritual experiences or encounters) too often takes precedence over loving one another. We preach the Kingdom, yet negate it by our doctrines: our traditions of men. But if anyone uses their interpretation of doctrine as the plumb line, then they have eliminated part of the body of Christ: the part that doesn't believe everything the way they do. Some will say, "But we must maintain truth!" Yes, we must. But what is truth? "Jesus answered,

We preach the Kingdom, yet negate it by our doctrines!

'I am the way and the truth and the life. No one comes to the Father except through me.'"[18] I'm sorry, but that verse does not say that people get to the Father by knowing the right doctrine. It says we get to the Father by knowing Jesus. Intimacy and love with Jesus is the key. Are there boundaries? Yes. Are there standards? Of course. But the Father's standards do not override His love for people.

Yet, rather than gather in love for one another and for Jesus Christ our King, we divide and separate from one another based on our interpretation of Scripture. If you're worried about truth, get to know the one who *is* Truth, Jesus Christ. Because in the end, it won't matter if you had the right doctrine. What *will* matter is if you had an intimate relationship with The One. "Many will say to me on that day, 'Lord, Lord, did we not prophesy in your name and in your name drive out demons and in your name perform many miracles?' Then I will tell them plainly, 'I never knew you. Away from me, you evildoers!'"[19]

Kingdom mentality does not divide brothers and sisters nor seek to dominate them. Kingdom mentality is based on relationship with and love for one another. Let Jesus work on other people's hearts and opinions; that's His and Holy Spirit's job, not yours.

Chasing after signs and wonders is not what we should be doing. Chasing after right doctrine is not what we should be doing. Chasing after Jesus in the Kingdom is what we should be doing!

> *Chasing after signs and wonders is not what we should be doing.*
> *Chasing after right doctrine is not what we should be doing.*
> *Chasing after Jesus in the Kingdom is what we should be doing!*

For many years I taught certain doctrines and believed that I was right and others were wrong. Then God showed me how wrong I was! It was an eye-opening experience to realize that the things I had pushed so hard were really not God's heart after all, but merely human traditions that seemed right in my eyes at the time.

I want to be an open book. I want Jesus to be able to mold me in any way He wants. But if I think that I know the best and only way to interpret Scripture, I can easily miss what Jesus really wants me to see.

This doesn't mean that I don't have opinions and beliefs about Scripture. And I will share them, if anyone really wants to know what I think. But I will *not* waste my time or anyone else's time trying to convince them that they are wrong. It's best simply to walk in humility and keep our hearts open to what Father may be showing us.

Our Father's Kingdom is built around the Tree of Life. Doctrine is based around the Tree of Knowledge of Good and Evil. The Tree of Life is about living in relationship with each other. The Tree of Knowledge of Good and Evil is about being right or wrong. Had Adam and Eve remained in relationship with God, they would have received all the knowledge they could ever want, but they would have learned it in the context of relationship. Instead, they chose to take it now and in their own way outside of relationship. Whenever we act in a way that puts knowledge and doctrine above relationship, we are operating out of the Tree of Knowledge, and the end thereof is not pretty.

> *Whenever we act in a way that puts knowledge and doctrine above relationship, we are operating out of the Tree of Knowledge.*

Sadly, many Christians, even Christian leaders, get this badly wrong. They seek after the power and knowledge more than the relationship.

I used to be that way too. But now I choose to love and work in relationship. When I'm in relationship with Jesus, I have all the Truth I can receive. And I trust Jesus that He's also giving those around me who are operating out of love and relationship all the Truth that they can receive.

Truth is not a divider. Truth is the God-man, Jesus Christ, who prayed that we would all be one. Unless you have a deep and abiding relationship with Jesus, no amount of correct doctrine will benefit you. The adverse is true as well: when you have a relationship with Him (who *is* Truth), no amount of *incorrect* doctrine will keep you out of the Kingdom. For it is Jesus Christ who saves us, not correct doctrine. Yes, we are to

> *Unless you have a deep and abiding relationship with Jesus, no amount of correct doctrine will benefit you. The adverse is true as well: when you have a relationship with Him (who is Truth), no amount of incorrect doctrine will keep you out of the Kingdom.*

judge things sometimes, but we must be extremely careful with how we judge, "for in the same way you judge others, you will be judged, and with the measure you use, it will be measured to you."[20]

Walking in sincere love and relationship are keys to growing into mature sons.

Chapter Three

The Three Plumb Lines

Something to unite, rather than divide.

On our journey of beginning Kingdom Equipping Center, the fellowship that Adena and I pastor, we often pondered which doctrines we should hold: doctrines that would unify us instead of dividing us. But when we asked Father which doctrines He wanted us to emphasize, for years we heard nothing. During this time our understanding of the Tree of Life versus the Tree of Knowledge continued to grow. Finally, when we were ready, Father began to download, not doctrines, but three plumb line attitudes that the Body of Christ can unite around. These three plumb lines immediately began to change our lives and the lives of those around us. And now many other churches and groups have adopted these as well.

The Three Plumb Lines are:
1. Jesus, The Way;
2. Love, Honor, and Respect;
3. Ask the Father.

These three plumb lines are the guide for uniting the Body of Christ. They start with and

---

The Three Plumb Lines:
1. Jesus, The Way;
2. Love, Honor, and Respect;
3. Ask the Father.

---

center on Jesus. Beyond these three fundamental principles we leave room for different interpretations of Scripture, while agreeing that Christ Jesus showed us the path to the Father and eternal life.

Now let's unpack these.

1. Jesus, The Way

Jesus said, "I am the way and the truth and the life. No one comes to the Father except through me."₂₁ "I am the gate; whoever enters through me will be saved."₂₂

"Whoever wants to be my disciple must deny themselves and take up their cross and follow me."₂₃

If we have personally encountered and engaged with Jesus, then a transformation is taking place within us, and it will be noticeable. The cross represents our willingness to lay down our lives to follow Him and walk in His ways rather than our own.

The bottom line of this plumb line is that we have chosen to dedicate our lives to follow and serve God the Father, Jesus Christ, and Holy Spirit as the one true God and creator of all things. There is no other god! And Christ's anointing is the only way by which we gain access to the Father and eternal life.

2. Love, Honor, and Respect

Many in the Christian community have committed their lives to Jesus, but they don't truly understand the fullness of the love of God. (To be honest, none of us do, completely.) But we must learn that **loving others** is the **most important** of all the commandments. "Whoever does not love does not know God, because God is love."[24] Our God is LOVE.

A teacher came to Jesus and asked him what was the most important commandment. "The most important one," answered Jesus, "is this: 'Hear, O Israel: The Lord our God, the Lord is one. Love the Lord your God with all your heart and with all your soul and with all your mind and with all your strength.' The second is this: 'Love your neighbor as yourself.' **There is no commandment greater than these.**"[25]

And this one: "By this everyone will know that you are my disciples, if you love one another."[26] How much clearer can Jesus make it for us?! If we do not truly love other people, then according to Jesus we have not even truly encountered God, not in a way that has allowed Him to change us so that we can love people like He does.

What God is doing is laying down the most basic and necessary guidelines (plumb lines) by which His children can lovingly work together. God has given each of us free will and a free choice. *Who are we, or anyone else, to think that we can take that God-given right away from someone?*

Consider this: Are there any two people in the world who have ever agreed 100% on everything? The answer is, absolutely not. Even those who think they do, if you dig long enough and deep enough you will find an area where they feel or think differently. This is part of the beauty of difference that God created within each of us. So why then do we demand that other Christians must believe exactly what we believe?

The fact is, you and I and everyone else are wrong in what we believe, somewhere.

But in the new Christian age that is now being ushered in, followers of Jesus will reach a level of mature sonship; we will display a highly developed level of love, honor, and respect for each other and our differences. We will come to understand that because the Father made us all different, then of course we will interpret some Scriptures differently. But in our new level of maturity, we will begin to see that most human interpretations are simply showing another wonderful perspective of our amazing and limitless God.

> *In our new level of maturity, we will begin to see that most human interpretations are simply showing another wonderful perspective of our amazing and limitless God.*

I expect to see mature sons who, as Paul said, "outdo one another in showing honor."[27] Imagine that! What if we could all do this one thing—outdo one another in honoring and respecting each other. That would change our entire world!

So how can we live this out?

When someone comes to me with a different understanding of a Bible text or fact, if they're fully convinced that the Word of God is saying something different from what I see or understand, that's their God-given right. God has not appointed me or anyone else on earth to have the final say on how to interpret Scripture. That's His privilege, not ours. I'm not the ultimate judge or policeman to decide if they are right or wrong; even popes from one generation to another have changed their view or interpretation of some Scriptures. The

Bible is God's Word to man, but our human interpretations are very fallible! And most of the time when we want to persuade someone to believe our interpretation, it's simply our pride welling up, wanting to be the "right one." So instead of arguing, now I listen politely to the other person, ask questions if something isn't clear, and then look and wait to judge the fruit of their interpretation.

What about when the other person believes something that I don't see at all in Scripture? So to me their view doesn't look like merely a different interpretation, but something that's actually extra-Biblical?

Well, I believe that everything in the Bible is true—but not *all* truth is in the Bible. Even the Bible itself says this, "Jesus did many other things … The whole world would not have room for the books that would be written."28

This is a crucial point. For instance, do we find computers in the Bible? No. But computers are true things that exist in our world. Is it true that cars can travel the roads at 60 miles per hour? Yes, but you won't find that truth in the Bible. It's actually rather absurd to think that our infinitely wise and infinitely creative God only ever wants to tell us what is written in the Bible: that He has nothing new to reveal to us. Especially when the

Bible itself says that He does! The Apostle Paul tells us so:

> "God's wisdom [is] a mystery that has been hidden.... None of the rulers of this age understood it... as it is written: 'What no eye has seen, what no ear has heard, and what no human mind has conceived...' God has prepared for those who love him."[29]

I guarantee you that what God has revealed about Himself in His written word is not even a drop in the ocean compared to what He has yet to reveal to us! God is infinite and eternal and cannot be contained! What a great deception of the enemy, to get us to try to stuff God into our little theological box. Instead, as we clearly see all through Scripture and Church history, the truth is that God is *constantly* revealing more and more of Himself and His ways to each new generation. If we get stuck in one interpretation from ages past, we may miss what He has for us today!

What a great deception of the enemy, to get us to try to stuff God into our little theological boxes.

So when someone has a different view of some aspect of God, or a different interpretation of some verse in Scripture, or believes some idea that I've never heard of or have always thought was incorrect, I don't get bent out of shape about it. If it's an important topic or idea, then I'll be a good Berean[30] and go honestly investigate their view and mine. I honor and respect the journey that God has them on and I respect their current understanding. After all, my understanding is only my *current* understanding. When God reveals more to me, my understanding expands!

To love, honor, and respect another person and their beliefs means that I am not going to try to force them to agree with me. *If* they are open to hearing what I believe, then I'll be glad to share it with them. But I hope I am not so arrogant as to think that my interpretation is the only right one! If I have the humility to understand and admit that I might be wrong, why would I want to push my personal beliefs onto someone else? Look for the people who are hungry to learn from you, and share with them. And be eager to learn from others.

> *I hope I am not so arrogant as to think that my interpretation is the only right one!*

Now this does *not* mean that I have to *agree* with someone else's understanding. Honoring, loving, and respecting are different than agreeing, and not all opinions are correct. But as long as that person holds Jesus as the only way to the Father, then they are in the same body as me. Why would I want to curse or hurt or demean my own body? That person is my brother or sister, so I will love, honor, and respect them in spite of any disagreement we might have. We are called to love even our enemies, after all!

Lastly, if for any reason you find that you went too far in a conversation, or did something that was wrong or taken wrong, and there is now a division between you and another part of the body —reconcile! If you can't agree or talk it through between you and the other party, find a third party to help you navigate through the dispute and come to some form of reconciliation. If you still disagree, okay, you disagree. We all disagree in some areas. But the most important thing is to love each other! Let there be no animosity between you.

Now when it comes to corporate meetings, some people will feel more comfortable gathering with like-minded people because certain beliefs are easier to discuss when you're with people of a like mind. That's okay. But please don't bad mouth, trash, or tear down others (including other denominations) just because they don't believe like you do! That is not the example of Jesus, and it certainly is not obeying His greatest command: to love others as you love yourself.

3. Ask the Father

"I tell you, the Son can do nothing by himself; He can do only what He sees His Father doing, because whatever the Father does the Son also does."[31]

This was Jesus's way of doing things, so it must be good. Jesus came to build His Kingdom in and through us. He built His church and gave us the blueprint. It's really simple. Ask the Father for His will, and then agree with Him: "*Your* kingdom come, *Your* will be done, on earth as it is in Heaven."[32]

We all probably know some things that are good things to do. But good isn't always the *best* —and Father knows best. Plus, He is doing things to bring us into an entirely new age. Since we don't fully understand what that looks like, if we're not careful, we could find ourselves fighting against God. (As Saul, later known as Paul, did.) And that is something you *don't* want to find yourself doing!

So may I suggest that we all start a new habit:

Don't do anything without first asking Father about it.

* * * * *

These are the three plumb lines.

Father said to me, "These three plumb lines will lead my people to a new level of love and maturity."

And we all need more love and more maturity if we are to grow to become mature sons.

Chapter Four

Engaging with the Supernatural & with Heaven

And God raised us up with Christ and seated us with him in the heavenly realms in Christ Jesus, [Eph 2:6 NIV]

One thing that all Christians believe—and they should, because it's crystal clear in the Bible—is that Jesus performed many mind-boggling, humanly impossible miracles.

What did Jesus do?

He Displayed Authority Over Nature

Calming the storm – Matthew 8:23-27; Mark 4:37-41; Luke 8:22-25

Feeding 5,000 – Matthew 14:14-21; Mark 6:30-44; Luke 9:10-17; John 6:1-14

Walking on water – Matthew 14:22-32; Mark 6:47-52; John 6:16-21

Feeding 4,000 – Matthew 15:32-39; Mark 8:1-9

Fish with coin – Matthew 17:24-27

Fig tree withers – Matthew 21:18-22; Mark 11:12-14, 20-25

Huge catch of fish – Luke 5:4-11; John 21:1-11

Water into wine – John 2:1-11

He Displayed Authority Over Sickness and Disease

Man with leprosy – Matthew 8:1-4; Mark 1:40-44;
Luke 5:12-14

Roman centurion's servant – Matthew 8:5-13;
Luke 7:1-10

Peter's mother-in-law – Matthew 8:14-15;
Mark 1:30-31; Luke 4:38-39

Two devil-possessed men – Matthew 8:28-34;
Mark 5:1-15; Luke 8:27-39

Man with palsy – Matthew 9:2-7; Mark 2:3-12;
Luke 5:18-26

Woman with bleeding – Matthew 9:20-22;
Mark 5:25-34; Luke 8:43-48

Two blind men – Matthew 9:27-31

Dumb, devil-possessed man – Matthew 9:32-33

Canaanite woman's daughter – Matthew 15:21-28;
Mark 7:24-30

Boy with devil – Matthew 17:14-21;
Mark 9:17-29; Luke 9:38-43

Two blind men – including Bartimaeus –
Matt. 20:29-34; Mark 10:46-52; Luke 18:35-43

Demon-possessed man in synagogue –
Mark 1:21-28; Luke 4:31-37

Blind man at Bethsaida – Mark 8:22-26

Crippled woman – Luke 13:10-17

Man with dropsy – Luke 14:1-4

Ten men with leprosy – Luke 17:11-19

The high priest's servant – Luke 22:50-51
Nobleman's son at Capernaum – John 4:46-54
Sick man at the pool of Bethsaida – John 5:1-15
Man born blind – John 9:1-41

He Displayed Authority Over Death

Jairus's daughter – Matthew 9:18-26;
 Mark 5:21-43; Luke 8:40-56
Widow's son at Nain – Luke 7:11-17
Lazarus – John 11:1-44

Who? Me?!

These miracles of Jesus are truly amazing and inspiring. But did you know that Jesus commands you to do the same? And He said that you could, if you truly believe. Jesus said, "Everyone who believes in Me will do the same things that I did… and even greater!"[33] Wow!

We know that every word Jesus says is absolute truth.

And we see that His words came true. The Bible records that uneducated fishermen like Peter cast out demons, healed cripples simply by telling them to get up and walk, and also walked on water. Philip was transported supernaturally across country.[34]

If you believe that the early followers of Jesus did miracles and had supernatural experiences like Jesus did (as you should), then you should also be willing to believe and accept that the God of the Universe (who dwells in you, don't forget!) has also given *you* unique abilities. It's something to think about, isn't it!

> **The God of the Universe, who dwells in you, has given you unique abilities.**

Other Mind-Boggling Miracles of Jesus

Jesus Walked Through People

> When they heard this, the people in the synagogue were furious. Jumping up, they mobbed Him and forced him to the edge of the hill on which the town was built. They intended to push Him over the cliff, but He passed right through the crowd and went on His way.35

Fascinating! How did Jesus do this without the mob seeing Him and stopping Him?

Jesus Was Transfigured

> After six days Jesus took Peter, James, and John with him and led them

up a high mountain, where they were all alone. There He was transfigured before them. His clothes became dazzling white, whiter than anyone in the world could bleach them. And there appeared before them Elijah and Moses, who were talking with Jesus.36

Here we see Jesus shifting from His normal physical body to something totally supernatural.

So here's a question to ponder: was this the first and only time Jesus did this? Or was it simply the first time He invited His disciples to *see* Him do it? We can't know for certain one way or the other, because it isn't recorded, but Jesus went away to pray by Himself a lot, and He said that He only did what He *saw* His Father in Heaven doing. So I suggest that this wasn't His first time at all. Why should it have been?

Was Jesus In Heaven and On Earth at the Same Time?

Jesus told Nicodemus that "no one has ascended to heaven but He who came down from heaven, that is, the Son of Man **who is in heaven.**"37 (Yes, I know: many Bible translations drop this phrase. Maybe because it's confusing or strange? But you can check the Greek for yourself: it's right there in black and white.)

So Jesus said, "I am in Heaven," even though He was seated in the physical world, right there with Nicodemus. Hmm; puzzling.

Angels Ascending and Descending From an Open Heaven

"[Jesus] then added, 'Very truly I tell you, you will see 'heaven open, and the angels of God ascending and descending on' the Son of Man."[38]

Hmmm? Sound familiar?

> He [Jacob] had a dream in which he saw a stairway resting on the earth, with its top reaching to heaven, and the angels of God were ascending and descending on it... He was afraid and said, "How awesome is this place! This is none other than the house of God; *this is the gate of heaven."*[39]

Do you see it? Jesus is saying that He is the stairway and the gate to heaven.

Jesus, not death, Is the doorway into heaven.

Jesus, Not Death, Is the Doorway Into Heaven.

We've all been taught that *death* is the gateway to Heaven. It is not. Jesus is. The Bible is very clear: death without Jesus will not get you to

Heaven, so death is *not* the door to Heaven. Jesus is the door. He is the only legal way in.

Jesus Himself said, "*I am the door.* If anyone enters by Me, he will be saved and will go in and out and find pasture."[40]

But what did Jesus mean when He said that everyone who enters through Him will go *in and out*? In and out of *what*?

Well, what is Jesus the door to? Jesus said that angels will ascend and descend on Him, in and out of Heaven![41] Jesus is the door to Heaven. Jesus is the Way! He said, "I am the way, the truth, and the life. No one comes to the Father except through Me."[42]

Jesus also came to tear down the wall of separation that previously kept us out of Heaven.

> When Jesus had cried out again in a loud voice, He gave up His spirit. At that moment the curtain of the temple was torn in two from top to bottom. The earth shook, the rocks split...[43] Therefore, brothers and sisters, **since we have confidence to enter the Most Holy Place** by the blood of Jesus, **by a new and living way opened for us through the curtain, that is, His body**...[44] Therefore, since we have a great high priest who has ascended

48

into heaven, Jesus the Son of God, let us hold firmly to the faith we profess... **Let us then approach God's throne of grace with confidence.**45 [*emphasis mine*]

In other words, the reason these things took place on earth and in the heavenly realm is so that you and I can boldly step into Heaven *while we are still alive on this earth!*

You and I can boldly step into Heaven *while we are still alive on this earth!*

That's what these verses in the Bible are saying. They aren't merely poetic, symbolic, or allegorical language. They are literally true.

WOW! Why has this not been taught??!!

Now I know that some of you are probably tempted to check out right now. "Hold on, Hodges," you're thinking. "If these verses really mean what you say, then why haven't we heard this before? Why does most of mainstream Christianity teach that we *can't* enter Heaven until we die? Surely this can't be true?"

Fair enough; let's think about this.

How many times have you casually quoted verses such as Ephesians 2:7 about being "seated with Christ in heavenly places" and Hebrews 4:16 about "boldly coming to the throne of grace" for help in time of need? How many times have you complacently read or heard preached Jesus's claim that anyone who believes in Him will do the same works He did? Most of us likely don't pause and think about what these verses might actually mean. But why are we so glib about them? Don't we and our teachers believe that they're true?

In effect, we've been taught that these verses are *not* really true. We've been taught that these statements in Scripture are merely poetic language.

In effect, we've been taught that these verses are not really true. We've been taught that these statements in Scripture are merely poetic language.

Why were we taught this? Why have these show-stopping verses been so downplayed and ignored?

I suggest it's simply because that's what our teachers were themselves taught.

Now don't get me wrong. I've had many teachers who helped me tremendously, as I'm sure you have. We should appreciate and respect them. But we can't forget that they are only human. As wise and learned and helpful and deserving of respect as they are, they are all—just like you and me—still only fallible and imperfect human beings. They make mistakes, as we all do. Sometimes big mistakes. So some of their teachings are also going to be imperfect and mistaken. The Apostle Paul even said so, in black and white: "we all see in part and know in part."[46]

So we shouldn't be shocked that our teachers make mistakes and unintentionally teach things that aren't completely true. It's the same with most of the doctrines and traditions we believe. For the most part, most Christians—and most Christian pastors and churches—have merely regurgitated what they've been taught, without thinking very critically about those teachings.

After all, it's difficult to teach what you don't believe or understand. And most Christians, including most teachers and pastors, haven't had a grid for the idea of visiting Heaven. It doesn't fit our normal everyday lives. And up until recently, there have been only a handful of people in each generation who have by faith stepped in.

But if we want to be good Bereans as the Bible exhorts us to be,[47] if we want our beliefs to be truly and fully Biblical, then sometimes we need to re-examine what we've been taught; what we say and do and believe. As Jesus himself said: "Be careful how you listen; for whoever has [a teachable heart], to him more [understanding] will be given; and whoever does not have [a longing for truth], even what he thinks he has will be taken away from him."[48]

> *...Whoever has [a teachable heart], to him more [understanding] will be given; and whoever does not have [a longing for truth], even what he thinks he has will be taken away from him.*

So what if some of these teachings on accessing Heaven have fallen short of teaching all the fullness that God intended? All the fullness that was intended by "[you are now] seated with Christ in heavenly places?"[49] That's all I'm suggesting. And it's not an illegitimate or incredible suggestion.

But now, God is revealing this truth to His people in masses, because it's time for the mature sons to rise up and take their place on earth and in Heaven.

Here's more Biblical evidence that we can visit Heaven.

Numerous times in Scripture, and all throughout history, there have been other people besides Jesus who stepped into or saw into the

Heavenly realms without dying. Job. Jacob. Moses (he saw God face to face, numerous times). Enoch. Elijah. Elisha. David. Isaiah. Ezekiel. Daniel. Stephen. John. Paul. Apart from Enoch and Elijah, whose final trip took them to Heaven with their body, all these others were evidently going to Heaven … in the Spirit. Hmmm.

And how about this: I think we would all agree that Heaven is not something we can see with our natural eyes or senses. One way to describe this fact is to say that Heaven is in another dimension.

But modern science has shown us that in this world we do actually exist intertwined with, or next to, other dimensions that we can't see. Jesus also taught this. He said, "Behold, the kingdom of God is within you."[50] Wow! How's that for a mind tweaker? The God and Creator of the Universe is a huge, enormous, unmeasurable being who exists across the universe and in every dimension He has created—and He's living inside you and me, right now.

So if the Creator of all these multiple dimensions lives inside you, maybe you're *not* limited to experiencing just this one dimension of existence?

If you are in Christ, and if He is in you and in the Father at the same time, then are you not also in the Father with Christ? And if Jesus is a gateway into Heaven, and you have Holy Spirit in you to help you communicate with the Father, then are you not also a gateway into the Kingdom, into Heaven, as Jesus was and is? Why not? Jesus said that He is the Door, and this Door is living inside you.

> *If Jesus is the gateway into Heaven, and Jesus is in you, are you not also a gateway into the Kingdom, into Heaven, as Jesus was and is?*

And where are you right now as you're reading this? Well, according to the Apostle Paul, you are also in Heaven *at this very moment*. "God raised us up with Christ and seated us with him in the heavenly realms in Christ Jesus."[51] This says that He *has already* seated us in Heavenly places. It does not say, "He *will*." It's already done. We just need to learn to believe this so we can operate there.

If you say that we can't see or engage with Heaven before we die, then are you not saying that death, not Jesus, is the doorway into Heaven? Death, not Jesus, is the only way we can access Heaven? Death, not Jesus, is the *only* way there?

Jesus walked on water and through walls and had Heaven open over Him—and He said that his followers will do *even more*. That means you and me, not only Stephen[52] and Paul and John. And they visited or saw Heaven, so why should us going into Heaven be so unexpected and hard to believe? Is it that far of a stretch? No! It should be fully expected, especially since Jesus is already there, now.

* * * * *

This has been an extremely abbreviated summary about engaging with Heaven. There is so much more you can learn from our online course called "Ultimate Impact." You can join it at www.KingdomTalksMedia.com. (The link is on the home page, under "Online Courses.")

Adena and I have also been teaching on this subject at our church in Colorado Springs. And it is changing lives! We've seen an increase of intimacy with Jesus like never before!

If that were all we ever got from it, it would be far more than enough! But we are seeing so much more power and authority beginning to be released. People are being set free and becoming what Jesus called us to be—His *Ekklesia*; His government on planet earth, which I'll talk more about in Chapter 7.

Chapter Five

Chapter Five

Your Imagination, part 1:

It's Not a Toy—It's a Key!

Christopher Carter, author of the fascinating book *Cosmic Shift,* does a fantastic job of sharing the journey of the development of the word *imagination* and also the idea of it, and how it came to mean what it means today. I love Chris and his humble yet deep concepts that he delivers while entertaining everyone. He's quite engaging. If you ever get a chance to see him at a conference, I highly recommend taking advantage of the opportunity.

Imagination—as an idea—did not exist in its present form when Jesus walked the earth. What did exist was the idea for the word *inspiration*. *Inspiration* carries the connotation that an outside source, a spirit of some sort, comes into a person and gives them ideas or thoughts: *in-spiritization*, we might say. In other words, if a person came up with a new or revolutionary idea, everyone back then thought it was due to a spirit from the outside coming into a person and *possessing* them with that idea.

However, after Jesus ascended into the heavens, He sent Holy Spirit. Holy Spirit came into those who invited him—but He didn't leave. Holy Spirit inspirited people with permission only, but then He stayed.

This is a shift that can be seen clearly. Before, the thinking was that a thought or idea, when it came, would come from the outside, into the inside of a person, and possess them with that idea or thought. After Jesus ascended and Holy Spirit came, suddenly men and women begin having new ideas and thoughts that came from within them, from the Holy Spirit.

If you're born again then you also have the Holy Spirit living within you. If you choose to, you can open yourself up to more and more of His leading. We call this "living from the inside out." As you begin to live from the inside out, to engage with your sanctified imagination, (i.e., your spirit-man) you will begin to move and operate in new ways. For example, you might notice that your level of wisdom begins to increase dramatically. This is God (Jesus/Holy Spirit) operating in you!

> ### *Your imagination and your spirit-man are one and the same.*

Your Imagination is Powerful!

I guarantee you, your imagination is not at all merely a child's toy nor a waste of time. God takes it very seriously. In fact, I'll be sharing in the next chapter how I believe very strongly that the imagination is only part of your spirit at work.

Here's one powerful example from the Bible.

In Genesis 11, Nimrod and his people are building the tower of Babel. God comes down to inspect their work. Notice this: it's *before* they are finished, but the text says, "the LORD came down to see the city and the tower which the sons of men *had built*."53 Now some translations will end that verse with the words "sons of men were building." However, that is *not* the correct translation of the *qual perfect* tense of the Hebrew verb. The qual perfect tense signifies a completed act, so the correct translation is *had built*.

This shows a powerful truth: once we imagine something, it is often as good as done. The Father certainly considers it so! "But I say to you that whoever looks at a woman to lust for her has already committed adultery with her in his heart."54

> ### *Once we imagine something, it is often as good as done.*

This is why it is so important that we *take every thought captive*, as Paul exhorts us to do: "bringing *every thought* into captivity to the obedience of Christ."₅₅ We tend to focus on correcting our (and everyone else's!) words and actions. But Paul focused on our thoughts: i.e., our imagination. Why? Because our imagination is such an amazingly powerful tool; it can completely change our own or someone else's life! It's like the Bible says: "as a man thinks in his heart, so he is [and so he becomes]."₅₆

> **Our imagination is such an amazingly powerful tool; it can completely change our own or someone else's life!**

Now we know that Holy Spirit resides in us. When you begin to connect with Holy Spirit to step into and engage with your existence in Heaven, you're working in conjunction with Holy Spirit to see or perceive Heaven. If you feel like you're making it up, as Chris Carter would say, "YOU ARE!" And that shouldn't shock you. After all, you are created in God's image, which means that you were created to create! With the help of Holy Spirit, you are engaging your spirit to interact with Heaven! I know this is a paradigm shift for many of you. But ask anyone who is engaging with Heaven and they will most likely tell you that they are engaging their sanctified imagination—their spirit—to do so. Paul's words suddenly make more sense when we understand that he's referring to our spirit: "I pray that *the eyes of your heart* [i.e., your spirit] may be enlightened."[57]

Some Hurdles

There are certain hurdles that tend to keep us from engaging with our imagination.

Some of you may be painfully aware of your unsanctified imagination. If this is you, then you need to go through some spiritual exercises with Jesus's blood to cleanse those unsanctified imaginations and get rid of them. However, when you begin stepping into the awareness of your existence in Heaven and operating in conjunction with Holy Spirit, you will begin to see a whole new world and level of the Kingdom.

Another common hurdle is that we think our imagination is untrustworthy, because we see children using their imagination all the time and we don't want to be thought childish.

But remember what Jesus said: "Assuredly, ...**unless you are converted and become as little children,** you will by no means enter the kingdom of heaven."[58] Wow! Let's unpack that. First of all, He starts off with a strong "Listen up! Take this seriously! It is true and faithful!" That's what *Assuredly* means. Then Jesus said that unless you 1) are converted (born again of the Spirit) and 2) also become *childlike*, you will not be able to enter and experience the Kingdom of Heaven!

Here's my interpretation of this.

If we aren't willing to be born of *the* Spirit so *our* spirit can come to life, we won't be able to experience the Kingdom of Heaven, because it's only in the spirit and by the spirit that we can enter into Heaven right now.

> *If we aren't willing to be born of the Spirit so our spirit can come to life, we won't be able to experience the Kingdom of Heaven, because it's only in the spirit and by the spirit that we can enter into Heaven now.*

Let this sink in, because it's crucial: your imagination and your spirit-man are one and the same. (I'll explain more of this in the next chapter.)

So I challenge you: Ask Holy Spirit. Ask Jesus. Ask Father. "How much does my spirit really do? Is my imagination just my imagination, or is it much more? How does it work? Why did you give it to me? What am I supposed to do with it?"

Stop Believing the Lies of the Enemy!

The enemy has temporarily won a battle over the Church by convincing us that, as Christopher Carter says, "Imagination is okay for children under 5 and adults over 70, but the rest of us need to stay grounded and logical and pay our taxes." We've been taught that our spirit—our imagination, the eyes of our heart—is just an impractical thing that gets in the way of "real life."

But ignoring our spirit is the complete *opposite* of how we're commanded to live!

"God is spirit, and those who worship him must worship [and pray and act and live] **in spirit** and in truth."[59] **"To set the mind on the flesh is death,** but to set the mind on the Spirit is life and peace."[60]

Too many Christians have bought the devil's lie: that they should devalue and disengage from their spirit and instead value and empower their soul and body. That they should eat the fruit of the Tree of Knowledge of Good and Evil, in other words. Just as he did with Adam and Eve, the devil has deceived far too many Christians into believing him instead of believing Paul and Jesus!

We must repent of what we call our (wise) skepticism but Jesus and the Bible call our (foolish) doubt and unbelief ("Oh you of little faith!"), and we need to pray as Elisha prayed for his servant: "Lord, please open the eyes of my heart so I can see the spiritual realities, not merely the physical realities."[61] (If you struggle with seeing, hearing or sensing in the Spirit, please check out our course Ultimate Impact to help you with this.)

If we can shake off religious spirits and our preconceived ideas and teachings that we accepted probably uncritically, and just for a few moments give Father the opportunity to show us something new and fantastic, we will find an amazing tool He's given us—a powerful spiritual tool to help us engage with Him much more clearly and directly and personally. And it's been right there in Scripture all along.

I know this is all true, because it happened to me.

I was a logical, Western-thinking skeptic for most of my life. But then I began to see through the deception that the enemy had fed me, that my logic and reason should be king in my life rather than my spirit. I then made choices to put aside my skepticism and doubt—i.e., always trying to find reasons why *not* to believe—and began to reason within my spirit to see how things might actually fit together.

As a result, my life has become so full of God-encounters that I will never go back. Not only are the spiritual experiences I'm having phenomenal, but much more important, my intimacy with Father has grown exponentially! I know Him now better than I ever have, and my love for Him is greater than it has *ever* been. If using my imagination while believing and understanding it to be my spirit does only that, <u>I'll sign up every time!</u>

I know Him now better than I ever have, and my love for Him is greater than it has ever been. If believing and understanding my imagination to be my spirit does only that,
<u>I'll sign up every time!</u>

Chapter Six

Your Imagination, part 2: A Deeper Look

Our spirit is responsible for so much more than we know.

I'm learning more and more that our spirit is so much more powerful than we currently understand. It's another one of those subjects where our level of understanding doesn't measure up to even a drop in the ocean of the full truth. There is so much more! The rabbit hole just keeps going deeper and deeper!

Sometime after I wrote the content of the previous chapter, God began to reveal to me new information. I want to help us break out of the lies that keep us from soaring, so I'm just going to come right out and say it. I've meditated on this topic and processed it many times over. This is what I believe Father is showing me; this is my new and current definition of the word *imagination*:

I'm serious. *Imagination* is merely a humanly created word that attempts to describe the work of our spirit from a secular mindset. It's evident from how we use it in our world today that we use this word to describe functions of our spirit. But the worldly definition of the word falls far short of describing the power of our spirit.

> *Imagination – "A word created by a secular world to describe functions of the spirit without admitting that there is a spirit."*

Here is the *Oxford English Dictionary*'s definition of *imagination*:

> A: "The faculty or action of forming new ideas, or images or concepts of external objects not present to the senses."
>
> B: "The ability of the mind to be creative or resourceful."

Think about it. Is there anything that we do with our imagination that isn't also performed as a function of our spirit? If so, I'd like to know what it is.

Is It from God or the Enemy?

Many Christians worry or are unsure whether things they are "hearing" and thinking, dreaming and imaging, are from God or from the enemy, or merely from themselves. And it's crucial to be knowledgeable and informed on this topic.

Adena and I teach a class on hearing the voice of God. We learned a lot on this topic from **Mark Virkler's teachings** and I highly recommend them. (Bless you for all your work, brother!) One of the important lessons to learn and understand when listening for the voice of God is how to tell the difference between His voice, your voice, and the voice of the enemy. It can be somewhat difficult, but with practice, you can learn it.

Here's an important but simple key.

If the voice you "hear" is telling you good things and building you and others up, that is probably God. (And sometimes you might find that you're talking to yourself. That's okay as long as it isn't aloud in a small group of people! Ha!) If that voice is tearing you down and condemning you and others, it is clearly the enemy. This is because Jesus is our Advocate and Good Shepherd and Holy Spirit is our Comforter and Encourager, while the enemy is our accuser. Plus, there is no longer *any* condemnation for anyone who is in Christ.[62] (Mistakes and need for repentance sometimes, yes; but condemnation, no. Jesus took all our condemnation on the Cross.)

Here's another key. Your body is a temple.[63] Your spirit lives in your temple. It's what gives you life. If you are born again, then you've also invited Jesus/Holy Spirit to reside in you. And like any building, the temple of your spirit has doors and openings that lead into it.

Now I would love to be able to say that once we open the door of our temple to Holy Spirit our work is done, but the evidence tells us otherwise. Being born again doesn't take away our freedom of choice, and God gives us the freedom to choose what spirit or spirits we want to open the door of our temple to. We can choose to let in any spirit we want; we have the ability to choose which spirits we want to let into us and work through us. So (often without realizing it) we can allow spirits of darkness and deception to operate in our temple. Now ideally, we don't and won't. But the hard truth is, we do. We let the spirit of fear in, the spirit of doubt, the spirit of anger; you name it. So Holy Spirit sometimes has to put up with a lot of crud we allow into our lives.

> *We have the ability to choose which spirits we want to let into us and work through us.*

We simply have to learn to kick out those other spirits that are not of God and repent for opening the door and agreeing with them. Thankfully for Christians this is relatively easy to do, since we already have the Spirit of Jesus living in us. (In Chapter 9 I'll share how I did this by engaging with the Courts of Heaven.)

Engaging with the Supernatural and with Heaven.

We can all engage with either the demonic or with Holy Spirit anytime we want. It's our choice as spiritual beings.

If people choose to engage with the demonic in one fashion or another, then they will see and hear things and go places that the darkness wants to take them. That's what witches, warlocks, and people engaging with the occult realm are doing. They are engaging their spirit with demonic spirits to gain power and experiences. But if you instead engage your spirit with Holy Spirit, then you will see things and go places in the heavenly places that Father God wants to show you.

Engaging with Holy Spirit makes all the difference, just as praying to the Father instead of to some man-made idol makes all the difference in your prayers. You might be using the exact same words and physical posture as some idol worshipper or follower of another religion, but that's irrelevant: it's whom you are praying to and in whose name you're praying that's important. It's the same with engaging with Heaven.

And you'll know if you're engaging/partnering with the darkness.

How? Simple. If you're trying to engage the spirit realm but you're not going through Jesus, then you're engaged with the demonic—so STOP! If you're engaging your spirit/imagination to solve a problem or view a vacation spot you're hoping to go to, that's probably just you using your spirit/imagination for yourself. And there's nothing wrong with that.

> ### *If you want to enter Heaven, Jesus is the way and He is the door.*

However, if you want to enter Heaven, Jesus is the way and He is the door. In our Ultimate Impact course we teach you how to safely engage your imagination/spirit so you can step into God's Kingdom. We teach you the Bible verses that show this is what the early disciples did and how it was actually an understanding that we (God's children) *should* engage with our Father in Heaven. This is not reserved for so-called spiritual giants. No! This is for you and me!

I can tell you, after doing this multiple times a week for months and now years, that there is nothing like it. More and more people are experiencing the same thing. It's amazing to hear someone else describe what they see in Heaven and realize it is just the way I saw it! There is so much more to learn about our Father's Kingdom, and we are only scratching the surface. I can say, after personally encountering thousands of people who are doing this, and seeing the intimacy they have with Father, Son, and Holy Spirit, that if that intimacy were the only thing that ever came of this, it would be so well worth it!

This whole subject may be way off your grid or out of your paradigm, and trust me, as a former skeptic, I understand. But I'm convinced that engaging with Heaven is a marker of those who will be helping the Church shift into the age to come. Almost everyone can sense that the Church as we know it is shifting. How that will look when it's finished, we don't really know. But we do know that from age to age we continue to grow in our understanding of God, and we know that He *always* reveals more of Himself to each new generation. We also know that the devil is not in the business of teaching people how to develop a deeper relationship with Father, Son, and Holy Spirit!

> **Engaging with Heaven is a marker of those who will be helping the Church shift into the age to come.**

So if we can get past the stigma and the deception that our imagination is childish or untrustworthy or "just a toy" and instead realize that the word itself is simply an attempt by secular minds to describe functions of our spirit without admitting that we have one, then we can make massive leaps into this new season that Father has prepared for us!

What better tactic of the enemy to keep us from our full potential than to convince us that our imagination is just a fluky daydream toy that will get us in trouble with our boss or teacher if we're not careful. No! Our imagination, our spiritual eyesight, is part of who we are as children of God and made in His image. Our imagination, our ability to engage with the realm of Heaven, is a gift to us from our Father! It's time we give it the attention it deserves.

> *Our imagination, our ability to engage with the realm of Heaven is a gift to us from our Father! It's time we give it the attention it deserves.*

We need to learn to intentionally engage with Heaven!

Chapter Seven

Becoming the Ekklesia

"Your Kingdom come, Your will be done, on earth as it is in heaven." [Mat 6:10 NIV]

Maturing Sons

If you haven't yet noticed, God's people across the planet are desiring **more**! God's creative power is rising up in each one of us. He is creating a desire to know Him at deeper levels than ever before. There is a yearning in His people to see "His Kingdom come, His will be done on earth as it is in Heaven."[64]

The age of Christianity being thought of as merely a ticket to heaven is passing away. God is breaking off the old and pouring out His last wine—the *best* wine—into a new wineskin. As He always does, Father is also giving us new mandates, new mindsets, new systems and structures, and new gifts for the new season that is upon us.

> *Father is giving us new mandates, new mindsets, new systems and structures, and new gifts for the new season that is upon us.*

And Father is looking for those who hunger and thirst for His righteousness and the fullness of His presence: those seeking His Kingdom first, above all else.[65] He is searching for mature sons who "attain to the unity of the faith, and of the knowledge of the Son of God, to a mature man, to the measure of the stature which belongs to the fullness of Christ."[66] These are the ones He can make kings and priests over His Kingdom. He's looking for "a *chosen* race, a *royal priesthood*, a holy nation, a people for God's own possession, so that [they] may proclaim the excellencies of Him who has called you out of darkness into His marvelous light."[67]

> *Father is searching for mature sons who "attain to the unity of the faith, and of the knowledge of the Son of God, to a mature man, to the measure of the stature which belongs to the fullness of Christ."*

But here's the kicker… **He's also waiting on *us*!** We have a part to play in this.

What is our part? What is the work of God that we are to do?

Jesus said, "The work of God is this: to believe in the one He has sent."[68] This work is both profoundly simple and profoundly difficult. For the most part, most churches and most Christians have limited their belief to a fire insurance policy and a ticket to heaven. But there's so much more to being disciples and the Body of Christ on earth than merely believing facts for our personal benefit—we have a divine mandate from Jesus Himself to disciple all nations and to be His government on planet earth![69]

> **Most Christians have limited their belief to a fire insurance policy and a ticket to heaven.**

We are now in a season of maturing and learning how to administrate from Heaven in order to see the things of Heaven change the earth; learning to see the pattern in Heaven and then bring Heaven to planet earth. So the Father needs people who are ready and willing to move into this new season with Him. What He did yesterday was only one step in our journey—He needs people who have the courage to take the *next* step with Him!

All of Heaven and everything in the earth is yearning for us to get our act together so He can do this. But we must understand: the maturing process is a laying-down process. When God's people lay down their own egos and agendas and rise to their place as mature sons operating as the *Ekklesia* (God's government in the earth), then we will begin to see our nations truly change; we will see things in our world becoming more and more like Heaven. This is where we are headed in this next season!

> **When God's people lay down their own egos and agendas and rise to their place as mature sons operating as the Ekklesia (God's government in the earth), then we will begin to see our nations truly change.**

Let's not forget: we are *not* fleshly beings who just so happen to have a spirit—we are *spirit* beings living in a body of flesh. We are citizens of the Kingdom of Heaven. Jesus taught us to pray, "Your kingdom come. Your will be done on earth as it is in Heaven."[70] On planet Earth we are to be ambassadors and representatives of the Kingdom of God. Jesus has given us the authority to act and be so.

Becoming the *Ekklesia*

Ekklesia was the name for the ruling council of the Greek (and later Roman) cities. Like modern-day parliaments, an *ekklesia* was empowered to make laws and decrees and binding decisions for their city, including even declaring war and peace.

The reason Jesus named the groups He was forming on Earth His *Ekklesia*, was to empower and commission them to act on behalf of His Kingdom: to legislate Kingdom principles into being in this physical realm. That's what *ekklesias* did in His day and what they should do now in ours.

So as followers of Jesus, if we don't like what we see going on around us, we must take action to change it. That's our right and our responsibility as His *Ekklesia*! But we must first get our marching orders from the heavenly realm. We first look into Heaven and engage there to see what Father is doing and saying, then we bring that reality onto the Earth by decreeing it with the authority that Jesus has given us as His representatives on the Earth!

How do we enforce our decrees? As we walk with Him in heavenly places and become *one with Him and His people* (as He prayed that we would), then we will grow to be more like Him. Our hearts will be knit together with Him and one another and we will reflect who He is on the earth. Then our thoughts and desires will be like His, and Heaven will then enforce our decrees.

Jesus came as a first fruit, an example, not only to show us *how* to do this, but to show us that the time was near when God would tabernacle within us and give us this same authority. That His fullness and power would one day be released in us! But also like Jesus, first we must be willing to lay everything else down at His feet. When we lay down our lives and our agendas, as Jesus did, to become mature mediators/reconcilers/priests—loving and putting others before ourselves and humbly taking our place in the body of Christ. Then signs, wonders, and miracles will follow us wherever we go, as they did the disciples in the days of the Early Church. Then Jesus will fill us with full kingly power and authority to represent Him as His Kingdom government on earth.

If we were to truly become the *Ekklesia* and represent our Father well, then His love, demonstrated by us and enacted through us, would run every other force in this world out of business!

> *If we were to truly become the Ekklesia and represent our Father well, then His love, demonstrated by us and enacted through us, would run every other force in this world out of business!*

Christian Unity and Humility

Pride and self-centeredness are the biggest killer of God's children becoming mature sons, kings, and priests.

We must have the Father's heart, as Jesus did. And the Father is not envious: rather, He rejoices in other's joy and is willing to give up everything (i.e., Jesus) to help them! We see an amazing example of this in the book of Acts, where the Christians had *all things in common*. "What's mine is yours, and what's yours is mine." Let that soak in for a moment!

How far are we from this? How far are we from being willing to lay down our lives for one another like that?

Well, how often have you said or thought, "Of course I'd give my life for you, my brother or sister, but I won't let you use my _____" (fill in the blank). "Of course I love you like I love myself, but my time and money is for me." I'll be the first to admit that I also struggle with this, but we simply cannot allow such prideful deception to continue to exist in us!

Praise the Lord, as I spend more and more time in Heaven with my Father, I am seeing my stony heart melt more and more.

We are called to lay down our lives for one another and be unified with one another as Jesus and the Father are. We must lay ourselves, our individual agendas, and our rights on the altar so that the Father can raise us up.

Priests and Kings

It's the Priest and King teaching all over again. We are called to be kings and priests of our God.[71] We are children of the King, called and adopted into His family, and all creation is groaning and waiting for us (all followers of Jesus) to be filled with the Spirit and fully mature: to become kings ourselves, under the King of Kings.[72]

But before the Father will give us Kingdom authority, we must learn humility through the priestly process. When we learn humility and love for others as a priest, then He will give us more kingly authority. Then we are given an opportunity to go low again into our priestly role. Once we learn the next lesson, He then gives us more kingly authority. It's a cycle of glory to glory, and this process goes on throughout our life.

> *When we learn humility and love for others as a priest, then He will give us more kingly authority.*

Our priestly role displays the love and compassion of God. We are called to mediate and be a priest for God and take up the role of reconciliation,[73] drawing humanity to Jesus. Jesus says we are to love our enemies. Are you willing to stand in the gap for your enemies? Jesus was.[74]

We must mature into a place where we are willing to stand in the gap as Esther did,[75] willing to give up her life for others. Esther acted as a priest. She stood in the gap and was willing to sacrifice herself to save her family and her people.

But too many of us want to, or think we can, jump straight into a place of kingship and decreeing, when we haven't yet learned to love others sacrificially or to walk in humility. But what is good and pleasing to the Father? "He has shown you, O man, what [is] good; And what does the LORD require of you but to do justly, to love mercy, and to walk humbly with your God?"[76]

We must start being the real *Ekklesia*! This can only happen as we are willing to ascend together, *as one,* into the heavenlies to see what our Father is doing, and then truly laying down our lives and our wills to accomplish His will on the earth.

Chapter Eight

About the Courts of Heaven

"The court was seated, and the books were opened."

For me, the Courts of Heaven were the single most productive part of my journey to emotional healing: to truly believing that the Father is on my side.

Only a few days into my study of the courts, I decided to give it a try. I was sitting at my desk studying the subject one evening when I felt compelled to take the situation of a close family member into the courts. This family member was in great need of getting work, but for weeks there had been no breakthrough. I understood that, in my role as a priest before God, I could represent another person or situation in the courts. I would mediate on their behalf and then, taking on my kingly role, I would come back to this earthly realm and begin to decree out as a king what I had seen or been told in the court. So, to the best of my knowledge and ability at that time, that's what I did.

I'm not exaggerating when I say that I had not even finished my decrees when my phone rang. It was this family member, and the very first words out of her mouth were, "Guess what? I got a job!" She was so excited! For my part, I wasn't sure what to think. I was somewhat dumbfounded, to be honest!

The very next night I was in my office again. Our church had been looking for a new location to hold our services. We'd been searching for some time, but without a breakthrough. So, in my priestly role, I took the situation before the Father in the courts. After I presented my case to the Father, I began to proclaim and decree it into the earth as a king. No exaggeration again, I wasn't even finished when my wife knocked on my door. "Guess what?" she exclaimed; "we have a place!"

As you might imagine, I was amazed.

But wait: there's more!

Two days later I took a work situation to the courts. The same thing happened! This time I hadn't even *finished* making my declarations when my phone rang. It was the guy I needed to talk to, and he already had the solution!

Has it always happened this way? No, but the percentage of answers is ridiculously aligned in favor of the courts being extremely effective! And at that time I had almost no idea what I was doing; I was a raw beginner—but this just shows the amazing power of the courts.

Our Father is Not a Legalist

If you research the Courts of Heaven online, you'll find many people teaching access to the courts in many different ways and with many different protocols. Some teachings on the courts have highly detailed tracks and, in some cases, situations where if you don't do everything exactly right, it's claimed that Father will make you start all over. This all has a resoundingly familiar tone of performance and measuring up that I just do not see as part of the true gospel of grace.

Adena and I have instead approached this topic from the viewpoint that Father is *not* trying to complicate things or make it difficult for us to receive His blessings. Rather, He has gone out of His way to make it easy for us, by creating many different ways for us to receive the blessings and benefits for healing and the abundant life that Jesus came to give us. Our Father wants us all to have all of these.

A distorted human "gospel" (actually the law, not the good news) tells us that we must be *worthy* of God's grace and that He will only reward us with the joy of His presence when we do everything right. However, the true gospel is that God is *Love,* period! "Whoever does not love does not know God, because God is love."[77] Paul says that Jesus came to set us free for freedom's sake. "It is for freedom that Christ has set us free. Stand firm, then, and **do not let yourselves be burdened again by a yoke of slavery**."[78]

> *A distorted human "gospel"*
> *(the law, not the good news)*
> *tells us that we must be worthy*
> *of God's grace and that He will*
> *only reward us with the joy of*
> *His presence when we do*
> *everything right. However, the*
> *true gospel is that*
> *God is Love...period!*

We are to be free from religious systems and overlords who tell us that we must believe and act the way they do. In many cases this can be a serious system of brainwashing. But Jesus said, "Come to me, all you who are weary and burdened, and I will give you rest. Take my yoke upon you and learn from me, for I am gentle and humble in heart, and you will find rest for your souls. For my yoke is easy and my burden is light."[79]

Also keep in mind that the Courts of Heaven are only one of many tools that Father has given His children to work with. Our experience has shown us that going to the Courts does benefit most people most of the time, but as they say, your mileage might vary. If you find the courts don't work for you, don't worry: you will find your freedom through other tools and means that Father has provided. The courts are not always the proper solution. Father does have something for you, and it will come and show itself to you when you're ready.

With that being said, here are the bottom-line basics that Adena and I have found to be profound and effective, and without having to jump through a bunch of legalistic hoops.

The Heavenly Courts in Scripture

First, let's look at the Scriptures. Are heavenly courts mentioned in the Bible? The answer is yes, we find them very clearly. Here's just one instance:

> As I looked, thrones were set in place, and the Ancient of Days took his seat. His clothing was as white as snow; the hair of his head was white like wool. His throne was flaming with fire, and its wheels were all ablaze. A river of fire was flowing, coming out from before him. Thousands upon thousands attended him; ten thousand times ten thousand stood before him. **The court was seated, and the books were opened.**80

What an awesome picture!

But are these courts for us or against us? Is God, the Judge of the earth, for us or against us?

Before I show you a Scripture for this, let's look at the word *judge* in the Hebrew, because there we begin to see the true purpose of biblical judgement. The word translated "to judge" in English is the Hebrew word *dan*. Since Hebrew spelling often leaves out the vowels, *dan* is written with just two letters, *dalet* (d) and *nun* (n). And the Hebrew alphabet began as a pictorial language, so here are *dalet* (𝘝) and *nun* ( ) as written in ancient Hebrew. Every Hebrew letter also symbolizes a word picture: the letter *dalet* is also the symbol for a door; the Hebrew letter *nun* is the symbol for "life." (It actually looks like a sperm cell: which is amazing in itself, when you consider that, as far as we know, people back then had no microscopes to see such micro-elements.)

Put this all together and we find that, in Hebrew, the word *judge* or *judgement* actually means "the Doorway to Life!"

So there's your answer:

> *In Hebrew, the word judge or judgement actually means "the Doorway to Life!"*

> The LORD is our judge, the LORD
> is our lawgiver, the LORD is our king; it
> is He who will save us![81]
>
> The Ancient of Days came and
> pronounced judgement in favor of
> the holy people of the Most High.[82]

Wow; God is so good!!!

Unfortunately, the Church has traditionally misinterpreted the entire concept of judgement and turned it solely into punishment—the exact *opposite* of what it was intended to be for believers! When we understand that the heavenly courts are in our favor and the judge is our own Creator and Father. WOW! What favor we have! We cannot lose!

The Lower Court

There is actually more than one court in Heaven. Here I'll discuss what many people call the "Lower Court": or "Family Court" or "Mobile Court." In this Court of Heaven, we see several main players:

The Judge – Father God (Isa. 33:22)
Our Advocate/Attorney/Mediator –
   Jesus (Rom. 8:33-34; Heb. 7:25)
Our Accuser – Satan (Rev. 12:10; Job 1:6-11)

> **Witnesses** – The great cloud of witnesses, Satan, Holy Spirit, and Us (Heb. 12:1)
> **Records** – Our books or scrolls (Ps. 139:16)

This court is one in which even Satan himself can appear as your accuser (as He did with Job). This lower court is also where Father exposes any darkness that we, personally and corporately, have somehow come into agreement with. Why is this important?

Agreements and Covenants

Agreements and covenants, formal and informal, are a massively important part of the lives we live in this earthly realm, as we all learn. A tiny, seemingly insignificant agreement—saying yes to someone when you should have said no—can change the course of your entire life. This is also true in the spiritual realm.

Any earthly agreements you've made, with anyone, are legal documents in the spirit realm. These can be simple agreements, which you might perceive in the spirit realm as just a few sheets of paper with your signature on them. In the physical realm you signed this agreement by your thoughts, words, or actions. Contracts are a little more serious and may be many more pages. But the concept is the same: by agreeing with the enemy, you gave him legal rights to have certain access to your life, just as earthly contracts give other people certain legal rights in our life.

> *By agreeing with the enemy, you give him legal rights to have certain access to your life, just as earthly contracts give other people certain legal rights in our life.*

Covenants are even stronger. A covenant is typically something we are proud of, so when we sign a covenant, the spiritual bond is very powerful. We might see or perceive this in the spirit realm as a large, beautifully framed piece of paper signed by us and the enemy.

Unfortunately, and without realizing it, far too many Christians live much of their lives in agreement with lies and entities of darkness. These agreements serve to keep their daily and spiritual journey in turmoil and chaos. How can this be?

It's simple, really. Like in the 1999 movie *The Matrix*, in this natural world we do actually live in a matrix that the enemy has created: not a physical matrix, primarily, but a spiritual, intellectual, and emotional matrix. This matrix is the web of darkness and lies that the enemy wants us to believe are true.

Throughout our lives we are all smothered and bombarded—via the internet, radio and TV shows, social media, news outlets, other people, the enemy's thoughts masquerading as our own thoughts—with the enemy's lies and negative, dark spirits. We all go through our daily routines in this invisible matrix of deception, oppression, twisted thinking, and ungodly desires and emotional reactions that our enemy is trying to get us to come into agreement with. These lies are all designed to keep us in bondage to fear, pride, and other deadly sins. These ungodly attitudes are not only spiritually (and sometimes physically) deadly—they are the polar opposite of Love. And they lead to the polar opposite of the abundant life available to us in Christ. Whenever you decide to believe one of these lies (often unknowingly and unintentionally), you have just come into agreement with Satan, and thus have placed yourself under his power and authority in that area of your life.

These agreements or covenants with evil might also have been made by your ancestors (such as swearing the ungodly vows and oaths of Freemasonry or other organizations or the occult), and no one in your bloodline has ever taken the time or known how to break free of them. Ancestral agreements can be the cause of children inexplicably being oppressed by, or developing tendencies toward, hatred, pornography, monsters, or any form of unrighteousness or evil for which there is no apparent cause in their physical environment. In the same way, the devil was given access to oppress all of humanity because of our ancestor Adam's agreeing with him and eating the fruit of the Tree of the Knowledge of Good and Evil.

My Testimony

For example, back when I struggled with depression I constantly thought, and often said to my wife, "I'm depressed."

Instantly, with those two simple words, I had come into agreement with the enemy of my soul. How? Because that thought didn't originate with me; Satan was the one who put that thought in my mind in the first place! By repeating his suggestion as if it were true, I unknowingly declared that I believed it *was* true.

My agreement then gave him the legal right to send an evil spirit of depression to me, and because of my agreement, that spirit had a legal right to influence my soul: the seat of my emotions and feelings. Once I had opened the door just that tiny bit to my enemy, I found myself unknowingly making a tsunami of other agreements with him. Not only did depression enter in, but it would bring with it other dark minions: frustration, fear, sadness, hopelessness, death, etc. How did they get the legal right to come in? I gave it to them. "I'm frustrated." "I'm scared." "I just want to die." Each one of those dark spirits knocked on the door of my heart, introduced themselves, and asked to come in. Rather than saying, "No, you can't!," and slamming the door in their faces, I agreed with them and stepped aside so they could enter.

"I Have Given You Authority"

Unfortunately, too many Christians don't understand the power they have to say "NO!" to the enemy and his lies. That was me. If this is you now, then take this to heart. To paraphrase Jesus's decree in Luke 10:19, "I have given you all power and authority over the enemy." If that is true, which I believe strongly that it is, then any power Satan has over me is only because I (we) gave it to him. You should read and memorize Luke 10:19 right now, start learning and meditating on your authority in Christ, and immediately begin to believe it and put it into practice! This is a powerful key to massive freedom and breakthrough in your life!

Any power Satan has over me is only because I (we) gave it to him when we agreed with him.

Our goal, and the Father's goal for us, is to break free of this matrix of lies and step into the fullness of who we truly are in Christ. This is why the Lower Court of Heaven exists. We engage for ourselves and others in this court for the purpose of 1) breaking off legal rights of darkness against us and 2) coming out of agreement with lies and dark entities that we or our ancestors have agreed with, knowingly or unknowingly.

Once I realized these truths, I immediately began going into the Lower Court several times a day and requesting that the Judge (our Father) judge me! "Judge me, Father!" Once I understood that He didn't want to judge me in order to punish or condemn me, but rather to remove from my life everything that was not of Him (so that I could live an abundant life), I was all in!

We Have the Power and Authority

In this earthly realm we all live in a matrix of darkness and deception, but…

In Christ, in the Spirit, we can walk in light and love and freedom! In Him we are complete! "In Christ you have been brought to fullness. **He is the head over every power and authority.**"[83] Hallelujah!

Life is a two-sided coin. On one side is this physical realm and matrix of lies where we often struggle to understand who we are, where we

96

came from, where we're heading, etc. The other side is the confidence and perfection that we see in Jesus. The great news is that we *are* complete in Him. The Greek word translated as *complete* in the verse above means "to make complete in every particular; to render *perfect*." In Christ we are *complete*; in Him we have *already* been *perfected*. Who you are in Christ is *not* who you *become*—it is already done! It is *not* a future projection of yourself. It is the *real* you, complete in Christ! So there is nothing to fear. You don't have to fear any darkness or any schemes of the enemy, or even death itself.

> **Life is a two-sided coin.**
> **On one side we live in this**
> **matrix... We're on the journey.**
> **On the other side we are**
> **complete and perfected in**
> **Christ. (Col 2:10)**

The goal of this life is for us to learn to love again: to become like our Father who is perfectly loving, as you are (in your spirit) in Christ at this very moment. It's a process, and in order to love truly and freely we must learn how to break out of the enemy's matrix of lies. We must learn how to come out of our agreements with his dark entities who have deceived us into mental and emotional alliances with them. These alliances only pull us farther into the darkness of fear and away from the light of love. The Courts of Heaven are a place to achieve this freedom.

The old paradigm, where we dress for battle and yell at the enemy as we fight him, has left a lot of people wounded and weary. I've found that operating in the Courts of Heaven is so much more powerful and effective! Once you understand this model, you do the work in the spirit in the Heavenly courts first. Then, once you have the legal right from Heaven, you already have victory on earth and you only need to go through the steps needed to claim your victory!

Personally, I've found the greatest freedom and power to break free of the enemy's matrix come through operating in the Courts of Heaven.

Chapter Nine

Operating in the Courts of Heaven

Steps to engaging with the courts.

Here are what I have found to be the main principles of the Courts. Beyond these, I think we are adding to what Father intended and making unnecessary hoops for people to jump through. I'm going to repeat myself a little here, but please don't skip this part. These truths are crucial for our lives, yet they are so ignored or not even taught in most churches; even if we do believe them, we can easily find ourselves sliding back into our old unbiblical mindsets.

Main Principles

1. **Ask** the Father to judge you. He will then reveal whatever needs to be corrected.

2. **Agree and Repent.** Be willing to accept responsibility and repent for whatever wrong you have done. Repenting removes the enemy's legal right to keep you in bondage.

3. **Believe and act on Luke 10:19.** Through Jesus we have all power and authority over the enemy. Therefore any power or authority that the enemy has in our life is only because we gave it to him, by somehow agreeing with him. Renounce all such covenants, contracts, or agreements, then ask Jesus to cancel and remove them with his blood and have faith that "it is finished!"

As I discussed in the previous chapter, our agreements are so powerful. And our thoughts, words, and actions tell us what or who we agree with. "The good man out of the good treasure of his heart brings forth what is good; and the evil man out of the evil treasure brings forth what is evil; for his mouth speaks from that which fills his heart."[84]

But praise the Lord, we have Jesus's decree in Luke 10:19 (emphasis mine):

"I have given you authority…
to overcome *all* the power of the enemy."

The logical conclusion of this statement is that any and all power the enemy has over us in our life exists *only* because *we* gave it to him. Jesus declared that *we* are the ones who have power and authority over Satan, so if he *does* have power over us in some area, then obviously we gave it to him. How do we give Satan power? By agreeing with his suggestions and lies. Jesus never agreed with him, though, and that's why He could make His statement, "[Satan] has no claim on Me [no power over Me nor anything that he can use against Me].85

> *Any and all power the enemy has over us in our life.... is only because we gave it to him, and we have the power to take it back.*

So how do we get out of these agreements? How do we take back the legal rights we have given to our enemy?

It's actually quite simple. We go to the Courts of Heaven. The basic procedure in the Father's courtroom is the same as the procedures in a fair and ethical court here in the physical realm. But there are also some significant differences, as you'll see.

Step 1: Ask the Father to Judge You

In the spirit, go to the courts in Heaven and see yourself standing in the heavenly courtroom in front of the judge's bench. Jesus is at your side. He's your defense attorney. Your accuser is your enemy. Satan and his minions are there on the opposite side, eager to bring forth their legal right against your life. Simply ask the Father, the Judge, to judge you.

We often would not want a human judge to judge us, but the Judge of the universe is our loving Father, so there's absolutely nothing to fear. While man's judgement, like Satan's, is often unrighteous condemnation, the Father's judgement is the Doorway to Life! We actually *need* the Father to judge us, so we can be set free—free from anything and everything that hinders us from growing closer to Him, from learning who we really are, and from experiencing the abundant life that Jesus died to give us.

> *We want Father God to judge us, so we can be set free from anything and everything that hinders us from growing closer to Him, from learning who we really are, and from experiencing the abundant life that Jesus died to give us.*

So simply say, "Judge me, Father." And trust Him.

Ask Father to reveal where you are aligned and in agreement with unrighteousness or deception of any kind. For example: with lies of the world or from the enemy; or with evil spirits of anger, discouragement, depression, etc.

Step 2: The Accusations and Evidence Against You

The Father will then reveal to you one or more unrighteous areas of your life. When He reveals these to me, I then ask, "What legal right does the enemy have to my life in these areas?"

At that point, watch and listen. Because the enemy will bring out every covenant, contract, and agreement that you or your ancestors have ever made with him in this area of your life, whether through actions, words, and thought agreement. You might see or hear your accuser state the facts of your guilt. I usually see these all piling up on the courtroom floor. You might even see multiple file cabinets filled with paperwork. The courts in Heaven are very thorough!

As you look at all the accusations and evidence which the enemy has against you, let the weight and impact of these agreements, contracts, and covenants sink in. It can be almost overwhelming at times, but never more than you can handle: our loving Father will never allow that.

Step 3: Plead Guilty

This is not a place or time to defend yourself. Why? Because in the Court of Heaven, the devil has no ability to lie. Even if he could, this Judge is omniscient; He cannot be fooled, and the enemy knows this.

Also, because of the finished work of Jesus on the Cross, you have already been forgiven, so you won't be condemned for your sins and failings.[86]

So simply agree with your accuser, because every accusation he makes against you will be true. Don't try to defend yourself or shift the blame. Accept full responsibility for all the sins and ungodly agreements that were committed by you or your ancestors, whether in thought, word, or deed. Even if you don't remember or don't see how it is possible.

Step 4: Repent (Change Your Mind) and Come Out of Agreement

Contemplate and feel the sincerity of your repentance for allowing these things in your life.

Next, announce to the Judge that you renounce and repent of these sins and agreements. (Remember: contrary to much Christian teaching and thinking, to repent does not merely mean to change your *actions*. Fundamentally, and most importantly—since our actions are only the result, or symptom, of our beliefs—to repent means to change your beliefs and intentions; to change whose opinion you agree with.)

Once you've repented by an act of your will, the Judge, your Father, has the legal right to *revoke* every charge against you: because you are no longer agreeing with those sins and lies. And once those legal rights are removed, the enemy is left powerless against you; he can never use those sins against you again! (Unless of course you later give him *new* legal rights—but I strongly recommend against that!)

Step 5: Ask Jesus to Eliminate All Agreements, Contracts, and Covenants

After making sure that you've fully repented and that you want all those things completely removed from your life, ask Jesus to eliminate them. Watch—perceive—in the spirit as Jesus walks over to where all the evidence is stacked. He might ask you, for the record, "Do you want me to eliminate all this from your existence?" My answer is always yes!

Watch as Jesus places His hands on the evidence. I've seen Him disintegrate the piles and heaps of paper in different ways. He usually pours out His own blood over them, and I watch in the spirit as all the evidence against me dissolves away, out of existence under the power of His blood.

When Jesus's blood disintegrates something in the spiritual realm, that thing is entirely removed from *all* of Creation! This includes from all dimensions, all realms, and all forms of time. There is no place in all of Creation for those things to exist any longer. They have vanished from your life and can no longer be used to hold you captive—not by anyone or any thing!

> ## When Jesus's blood disintegrates something in the spiritual realm, that thing is entirely removed from all of Creation!

After this, the decree and verdict from the Father is, "YOU ARE FREE!"

You now have a clean slate, and the enemy's legal right against you is gone forever in those areas; hallelujah!

Step 6: Repeat As Necessary

If you should ever accidentally open the door again to an entity or lie that you don't want present in your life, simply repeat the process above. There is no condemnation because you made a mistake and accidentally let the enemy in. Simply cancel your agreement quickly. As you get proficient in the courts, you can easily deal with an agreement even while in the middle of work or play or anything else. You can, quite literally, go in and out of the courtroom in seconds. It's a quick trip in the spiritual realm!

The instant you realize that you've agreed with a spirit of anger, depression, discouragement, etc., or a lie such as "I'm not good enough", "I hate myself" ... STOP! Go instantly to the courts and get that thing off you! Repeat this process as often as necessary to get yourself free of anything that is not of God.

> *The instant you realize that you've agreed with a spirit of anger, depression, discouragement, etc., or a lie such as "I'm not good enough," "I hate myself" ... STOP! Go instantly to the courts and get that thing off you!*

Dealing with Your Triggers

Once I started practicing these principles, I quickly saw results. I was free ... until sometime later, when I would be triggered by something. Then I would agree with the darkness and give the enemy legal right to me, again. It was so frustrating!

For example, I used to be extremely sensitive about our finances. When our finances were okay, I was okay. But when our finances were challenging, this would trigger in me a response of fear, discouragement, and depression. I would immediately agree with those dark spirits. This opened the door to my soul and gave them legal right to come back in. I would go back to the courts and repent and get free again, but I wanted to know how to stop the vicious cycle.

I asked Jesus about this, and He pointed out that our brains have neural pathways. These physical connections in the brain are the result of natural and habitual responses that we've learned, in response to outside or internal stimuli.

Jesus first gave me a vision and showed me how to clear the neural pathway. He also led me to neuroscientist Dr. Caroline Leaf's teachings about these pathways. Some are small, but some are like superhighways. We have been so conditioned in certain areas to respond in specific ways (such as my example above) that our brains have developed massive neural pathways. Once we get rid of those, we will likely find highways and other roads, back streets, and paths that are associated with that superhighway. But the beautiful thing is that once you deal with the superhighway, the others are suddenly much easier to deal with.

Jesus taught me to pray in this way: "Gil, ask for My blood to eliminate the neural pathway that deals with the specific trigger you're experiencing. Start at the beginning neuron of that neuron pathway and everything leading up to that beginning neuron. Eliminate that neuron and everything from it all the way to the end neuron, and everything leading away from that end neuron. Ask me to completely eliminate that neural pathway out of your brain."

I did this, and it would work for a short season: days or few weeks before it would return. So I once again became frustrated. Why was it returning?

Well, Jesus had only given me what I asked for and what I could understand and handle at the time. When I then asked Him why these issues were returning, He gave me the rest of the prayer, which I would not have had a mental grid for when He gave me the first part. This is what He shared:

"Gil, it's like when you get a virus on one computer and it infects all the computers you have synced to a cloud. If you only eliminate a virus on one computer but not the others, eventually, because they're all connected through the cloud, that same virus is going to come back. Well, you actually exist in many places at the same time. For example, you are here receiving this revelation in the earth realm, while at the same time you are seated with Me in heavenly places. You exist in more than one place at one time; there are more instances of you than you know. Some of those you's in other realms (multiverses) struggle with similar or the same triggers. Yet you are all connected in the Spirit. So let me add to the original prayer what will finalize the destruction of that trigger, once and for all."

Jesus then gave me the rest of this prayer. "Father, please completely eliminate this neural pathway out of my brain in every form of my existence in all of creation: from every dimension, every realm, and every form of time."

DONE!   (I'll give the prayer in its entirety at the end of this chapter.)

I've shared this prayer with many people who have been set free by using it to stop the trigger patterns in our brains.

My triggers for that superhighway were now gone. Something similar might pop up, but not as bad as the superhighway. These were the highways, roads, backstreets, and pathways associated with the major superhighway. They were similar but much weaker, so easier to deal with, because the superhighway had already been dealt with. They took time and were a bit of a nuisance, but they needed to be dealt with as they came up, or they too could become superhighways. But with each one, it got easier and quicker until they were all wiped out of my existence.

Could they come back again? Only if I take the time to recreate those pathways and choose to agree with them again. So my advice is … DON'T!

My Experience

Learning how to take advantage of the Courts of Heaven set me free from nearly all my major struggles, depression being the greatest of these. As I described in the Introduction, depression had haunted me all the days of my life. There wasn't a time in my life where I don't recall battling with depression at one level or another.

If life were a lake or an ocean, then above water would be complete freedom from depression, while underwater would represent some level of depression. Until I was set free, I spent almost my entire life under water. On my good days, I battled low-level depression; on my bad days, I battled with a desire for death. On very rare occasions I managed to get my nose barely out of the water. I would desperately gasp a taste of freedom before I inevitably went back under. Those moments of relief came maybe once or twice a year, but never for more than a few days.

Two or three times a year I would go on what I would call "deep sea dives." These were times when I would see myself slide deeper and deeper into depression, usually spiraling down for days or weeks at a time. During those times I would go into hiding while my wife covered for me, because I couldn't be around people; I simply could not function. The shame I felt was too much—the shame of merely being me; of simply existing.

But praise God, through learning how to operate in the Courts of Heaven, I was set free.

Until several months later.

It was a Sunday. All day long I had felt a sense of depression coming over me, and I (foolishly) allowed myself to become discouraged. Of course it then came on even faster.

By that evening, the spirit of depression was hitting me hard. But it was time for our fellowship's Sunday night service, so, out of duty, I drug myself there. I made a short welcome speech, opened the service, and immediately walked straight out of the building. I simply left and went home, leaving Adena to handle the rest of the evening.

The next morning, I got up and drug myself to the gym. But I was so distressed and distracted by the depression and hopelessness in my soul that I was merely going through the motions of my workout.

Then Father broke through to me.

"Are you going to practice what you preach?" I felt a little embarrassed. I knew what He meant. I had begun teaching on my new revelation, that if a dark spirit is oppressing you, rather than trying to fight it, simply go to the Courts of Heaven and repent for what you have agreed with. Repent! Joyful repentance is realizing that each time you repent you are taking a legal right out of the enemy's hands and freeing yourself from his garbage. Take away his legal right and you'll be free!

> ***Joyful repentance is realizing that each time you repent you are taking a legal right out of the enemy's hands.***

But our enemy is subtle. He had crept into my thoughts so smoothly and quietly that I had begun to agree with him, without realizing what I was doing. "I'm feeling a little down." Agreement! Legal right given! Just a little bit at first. I was so convinced that I was rid of my depression for good, and so overjoyed over this, that I hadn't realized his stealth tactic of sneaking back in, quiet step by quiet step. He was so subtle that I didn't notice until he had full legal right (agreement) from me.

So when Father asked me if I was going to practice what I was preaching, It hit me like a ton of bricks. To be honest, I had to admit to myself and Father that I actually wasn't sure. Because while my mind and soul were smothered in the enemy's darkness of depression, my judgement was clouded. But then I thought, "I'll try it. After all, it can't hurt, and it will be wonderful if it works."

So right there in the gym, I engaged the spirit of depression. I actually invited it to jump on my back. "You want a piece of me, then go ahead: jump on my back!" If he wanted to take me down, he was going to have to fight me: but I was ready.

Now I had learned that entities of darkness cannot exist in the glory of Father's Kingdom, but in the spirit I can. When Depression jumped on my back thinking he was going to get a big piece of me, I immediately shot up in the spirit, straight up to the Father's throne of grace. (We are told to go there boldly, after all!) Game on!

Father was waiting for me and expecting me. He was sitting on His throne looking directly at me when I appeared before Him. And as soon as I crossed the threshold into His Kingdom, I felt Depression disintegrate and disappear. At least it seemed that he was gone, but I wasn't completely sure. Father looked me straight in the eye. He didn't say anything, but I could see that He knew I wasn't fully convinced. Immediately, He spoke to an angel who was standing near me: "Take him higher!"

The angel stepped up to me, wrapped his arms around me and then shot straight up into the air. We were going higher and higher into the glory light of Father's Kingdom. As we were going up, the angel said to me, "Yeah, you have to watch those open doors."

Suddenly, everything clicked and I understood it all. I had allowed the enemy an inch (subtly introducing his thoughts into my mind), and he had taken a mile. I had agreed with him little by little, until he had a full hold.

I knew then what I had to do. "The courts! Take me to the courts!" I cried out.

The angel immediately turned and headed for the Lower Court. When I arrived, Father was already waiting there, ready to go. Immediately, the enemy brought out all the agreements, contracts, and covenants from my family's bloodline. They were stacked high on the courtroom floor. I wasn't fighting just my own battle, but the left-over DNA record that I had inherited from my ancestors.

I quickly repented for agreeing with the enemy. I had sided with him in discouragement, sadness, and finally depression. I repented for myself and my family bloodline for agreeing with these dark entities.

Jesus then stepped over to the pile of records and put His hands over them. His blood poured from His hands, and as it came in contact with those records, I watched as they disintegrated out of existence, and I was free. I could literally feel it in my body in the natural, as well as the spiritual—I WAS FREE! And I've been free ever since, hallelujah!!

"The Blood of Jesus Prayer"

Jesus, I ask that your blood eliminate the neural pathway that deals with [name the specific trigger you're experiencing]. Start at the beginning neuron of that neuron pathway and everything leading up to that beginning neuron. Eliminate that neuron and everything from that neuron all the way to the end neuron, and everything leading away from that end neuron. Completely eliminate that neural pathway out of my brain, forever more. Blood of Jesus, please completely eliminate this neural pathway out of my brain in every form of my existence in all of creation: from every dimension, every realm, and every form of time. Amen.

Afterword

I've learned so much in recent years about my true value and who I really am, praise the Lord, that the enemy no longer wastes much of his time trying to get me depressed. I'm not trying to brag: it's just that I've grown much more sensitive to his approaches and when he's searching for a crack in my armor, and he knows that I know what he looks and feels like. When he does come around, he can be turned away with ease, thanks to our Father and the powerful tool He has given us all—the Courts of Heaven.

But this story is not only about me—it's also about you! You have an incredible part to play in this amazing Creation of our Father's! No matter what you've been through or what you are feeling currently, there are solutions to help you walk out the fullness that God has for you.

Each person is unique, so there's no one-size-fits-all answer. The way that I found freedom might not be yours. However, our loving Father does have a healing pathway for you. We encourage you to join the Ultimate Impact course and/or a course my wife and others teach called "Transformations – Becoming Who You Are."

You can also check out the free resources on our main website: www.KingdomTalksMedia.com and our Kingdom Talks online community at: www.Kingdom-Talks-Media.mn.co (that's right, there's no 'm'). It's free to join our community. This is where you can discuss and share and question with other followers of Jesus who are also on this journey of discovery.

A word from my wife, Adena:

The changes in my husband, Gil, have been truly remarkable since we began this journey of engaging with the heavenly realm. The first twenty-five years of our marriage were very challenging; there were times I wasn't sure we would make it. On our journey, it looked like Gil was the only one with a problem, while I seemed the perfect wife who heroically and sacrificially held things together. However, as he began to experience healing, that created a safer place for me to explore my own healing journey and to realize the ways in which I had contributed to the challenges we faced. I'm so grateful to Father that we both stuck it out and now can experience the joy of our life together!

We bless you in your continued journey of discovery, healing, and joy! Father has so much more for us than we could ever ask or think! No matter how stuck you might feel, there is a way through! Feel free to connect or ask questions by emailing us at *info@kingdomtalksmedia.com.*

SCRIPTURE REFERENCES

1 Eph. 2:6

2 Heb. 4:16 NKJV

3 1 John 4:8 NIV

4 Matt. 22:37-39 NIV

5 John 13:34-35 NIV

6 Luke 9:23 NIV

7 Isa. 55:8-9 NKJV

8 See Psalm 139:16

9 Gal 5:1 ESV

10 1 Tim. 6:10 ESV

11 Eph. 4:11-16 ESV

12 John 14:12 NIV

13 Matt. 22:37-38 NIV

14 Mark 16:17-18 NIV

15 Matt. 6:33 NIV

16 John 13:35 NIV

17 1 John 4:16-20 NIV

18 John 14:6 NIV

19 Matt. 7:22-23 NIV

20 Matt. 7:2 NIV

21 John 14:6 NIV

22 John 10:9 NIV

23 Mark 8:34 NIV

24 1 John 4:8 NIV

25 Mark 12:28-31 NIV

26 John 13:35 NIV

27 Rom. 12:10 ESV

28 John 21:25 NIV

29 1 Cor. 2:7-10a NIV

30 Acts 17:11

31 John 5:19 NIV

32 Matt. 6:10 NIV

33 John 14:12

34 Acts 8:39-40

35 Luke 4:28-30 NLT

36 Mark 9:2-4 NIV

37 John 3:13 NKJV

38 John 1:51 NIV

39 Gen. 28:12,17 NIV

40 John 10:9 NKJV

41 John 1:51 NIV

42 John 14:6 NKJV

43 Matt. 27:50-51 NIV

44 Heb. 10:19-20 NIV

45 Heb. 4:14,16 NIV

46 1 Cor. 13:12

47 Acts 17:11

48 Luke 8:18 AMP

49 Eph. 2:7

50 Luke 17:21 KJV

51 Eph. 2:6 NIV

52 Acts 7:55-56

53 Gen. 11:5 NKJV

54 Matt. 5:28 NKJV

55 2 Cor. 10:5 NKJV

56 Prov. 23:7

57 Eph. 1:18 NIV

58 Matt. 18:3 NKJV

59 John 4:24

60 Rom. 8:6 ESV

61 See 2 Kings 6:13-17

62 Rom. 8:1

63 1 Cor. 6:19

64 Matt. 6:10

65 Matt. 6:33

66 Eph. 4:13 NASB

67 1 Pet. 2:9 NASB

68 John 6:28-29 NIV

69 Matt. 28:18-19; Acts 1:8

70 Matt. 6:10 NKJV

71 Rev. 1:6; 5:10

72 Rom. 8:14-22

73 2 Cor. 5:18

74 Rom. 5:10

75 1 Sam. 25:23

76 Mic. 6:8 NKJV

77 1 John 4:8 NIV

78 Gal. 5:1 NIV

79 Matt. 11:28-30 NIV

80 Dan. 7:9-10 NIV

81 Isa. 33:22

82 Dan. 7:22

83 Col. 2:10 NIV

84 Luke 6:45 NASB

85 John 14:30 AMP

86 Rom. 8:1

Ministries of
Kingdom Equipping Center
Include

- **Kingdom Equipping Community**
- **Kingdom Talks Media**
- **Ultimate Impact**
- **Transformations – Becoming Who You Are**
- **Meditate on Me**

_____

Reach us through:

Kingdom Talks Media Website: https://kingdomtalksmedia.com/

Ultimate Impact (Course): https://kingdomtalksmedia.com/product/ultimate-impact-discipleship-course/

Transformations – Becoming Who You Are (Course): https://kingdomtalksmedia.com/product/transformations/

Meditate On Me (Guided Meditations): https://kingdomtalksmedia.com/product/meditate-on-me-monthly-subscription/

_____

Social Media

Kingdom Talks YouTube: https://www.youtube.com/channel/UC4xa71S16UE8U4TEnwWCYSA

Kingdom Talks Facebook Page: https://www.facebook.com/kingdomtalksmedia

Kingdom Talks Facebook Group: https://www.facebook.com/groups/kingdomtalksmedia

_____

Email: info@KingdomTalksMedia.com

Phone: 719-464-4873

Made in the USA
Coppell, TX
08 February 2023

12359815R00079